BATTLE RATTLE

PRO DEO ET PATRIA

CHAPLAINS UNITED STATES ARMY

Rev. Wallace M. Hale

Timberwolf Press

FORWARD

Once upon a time I was in a war that changed my world. I was with thousands of civilians as they trained for war, when they went to war, and when they fought a war. I was a regular army (Professional) Chaplain who tried to use his religious experiences and knowledge to build men up. I was young, virile and unconquerable. I stood for fairness, for justice, and for forgiveness in an organization that, at times, tried to ignore these concepts; my greatest asset was that I wanted to do anything possible to help the individual soldier and the unit. I wanted my chapel to be as well equipped as any other office in the outfit, and I wanted my chapel to be as comfortable as the officer's club or the NCO club.

For five years I preached, counseled and fought for individuals at every opportunity in this one infantry division; I decided to entitle these memoirs *Battle Rattle* for, to me, this soldier's term best described the mental trauma engendered in the human brain by persistent and extended hand–to–hand combat. Often the soldier suffered "Battle Rattle" when he realized he was one of the few men left standing—and somewhere close by there was a deadly bullet with his name on it.

TABLE OF CONTENTS

1
The Molding Pot

The sweaty, tired, disheveled khaki–clad kids were trying to debark from the troop train that had just pulled into this God–forsaken place called Camp Gruber, Oklahoma. They didn't know it was the former home of Bonnie and Clyde, the notorious two-member gang that terrorized lawmen and bankers in the Southwest.

Right now, it could have been—or might be— Singapore or Tibet as far as they were concerned. They knew their neighbors had drafted them to fight some unknown enemy of America who resided in some strange place called Japan or Germany. Their immediate problem was to get back on terra firma with their barracks bags, form into a line for the sergeant, and then get some place where they could be more comfortable.

This group of five hundred former civilians formed the first raw ingredients for the nation's first draftee division in World War II; and they had just met their first real enemy: the Oklahoma sun at midday.

The troop train had been jammed with men. Their uniforms were soggy with their own perspiration. They were already whittled down to peanut size by the long and uncomfortable train ride. Now, the troop sergeant calls to them to get into line and stand at attention on the 100–degree dirt siding. Daniel's fiery furnace couldn't have hurt much worse as they were readied for the trucks bearing down on them. They were learning the first major lesson of their military lives: The military has schedules that must be met. Troop trains cannot be held up. Tracks have to be cleared for the fourteen thousand other recruits who will soon be standing right here with little regard for the weather or their physical convenience or their present or previous states of minds or desire. "You're in the Army now— and we will mold you to our specifications."

I was their Chaplain and, whether they knew it or not—or if they ever cared, the U.S. army had given me a commission to be their spiritual leader in whatever they would face in the months and years to come. I was one of those Baptists who had come from the Bible belt in East Texas—but as one of my Baptist friends described his upbringing: "I was brung up on the belt buckle."

My preacher thought that he was an Old Testament prophet, but I had decided I wanted to be a shepherd and helper—not a guy who preached damnation; I wanted to live down in the world where men lived. I had become a regular army chaplain after six years of preparation. I was now a captain and an assistant division chaplain.

I had grown up on a farm, working twelve to fourteen hours a day at full tilt. I could bring a bull to full stop by hitting him on the nose with a fist. I could ride a wild bronc, had played a little football at Baylor University and had been encouraged to consider the army chaplaincy by a first lieutenant running a CCC camp.

Finally, I am here helping get a division ready for war.

***

My stories are about me in the 88th infantry division. I was very immature at times, but I managed pretty well. When I began this account, I was barely twenty–seven years old and had had three years of active duty. When I reported to Fort D.A. Russell, Texas (Marfa) in 1939, there was no Chaplain's school and since there was no other chaplain on the post, I had no one but my officers and enlisted men to teach me about regular army customs and procedures.

I was ordered to report in uniform. I put my first insignias on by looking at an infantry officer's uniform in a military catalog. I came on duty with a rank of first lieutenant and heard a few comments from captains who had served twelve years in grade.

There were some Thomason Act Lieutenants training at the post. I started going to school with them. I soon learned how to sight, aim, and fire a 155mm Howitzer, but I wore the wrong color of braid on my cap until a major with eighteen years service told me red was for field artillery and I was supposed to wear black. I wore my winter uniform in July to bury an officer. The commander called me in and I informed him I wasn't burying anyone while wearing a pink shirt and trousers, even with a Sam Browne belt on.

All in all, I got along pretty well. I didn't claim to be a West Pointer—I was a protestant chaplain who wanted to help everyone I could. I chaired the Army Relief Fund, acted as post librarian, edited the post paper, served as assistant athletic officer, ran the PX on maneuvers—and conducted religious services and spiritual counseling at every opportunity. I taught Sunday School classes, ran talent shows and had programs for the children. I worked out a deal with local ranchers to furnish a big bull for a community barbecue once each month.

When I arrived at Marfa, there were signs on restaurant doors discouraging soldiers from coming in, but gradually post and community relations improved. The old sergeants were my greatest supporters, and they helped me become a soldier—which wasn't easy—for I didn't have the mental makeup or the background to even understand the old military mind.

***

The commander heard I was getting married, and I think he thought it would be a good idea if I didn't live too close to the second lieutenants—so he gave me an adobe house. The quartermaster gave me all the furniture I needed, and I was assigned a striker. I caught him stealing money and put him in the guardhouse where I preached to him every Sunday afternoon. When he did his time, I took him back as a striker.

***

One winter morning, I started to the office and a cold Texas norther hit me in the face. I had ordered an army short coat from Lauterstein in San Antonio, but it had not arrived. I reasoned that I was cold and I needed an overcoat. I went into my closet and dragged out a grey–plaid civilian overcoat and put it on over my military uniform.

It so happened that I had an early appointment with Captain Stew Crawford. He was now adjutant, but wanted to take me down to show me around Battery C, an outfit he had commanded. I went to his office and saluted. Stew took a careful look, asked me to take off my coat and sit down. In an unruffled manner, he told me how the Battery was organized and staffed. Then he suggested we leave my civilian overcoat there and we went by his house. He gave me a long military overcoat he had gotten at West Point, hunted up some old insignias and told me I could wear it till mine arrived.

(In the years to come, the overcoat incident bothered me. It was such a silly and unmilitary act; I could imagine Stew telling his drinking buddies about that stupid chaplain. Years passed. I had become a lieutenant colonel working in the Pentagon. One day I spotted Colonel Stew Crawford coming toward me. There were happy greetings and we headed for one of the coffee bars. As we reminisced, I confessed my continued embarrassment about my stupidity. Stew claims he didn't remember the incident—and that's how I became soldier chaplain—I had lots of help and lots of real friends.)

***

I received orders to proceed to the Philippines, but Pearl Harbor happened five days later. I was naïve enough to be unhappy that the Japanese started the war before I could get there, but I quickly was assigned to Fort Gruber, Oklahoma, to become assistant division chaplain of the 88th Infantry Division—the first selective service division to be organized after Pearl Harbor.

***

For some reason Joe Rhoan remained front and center, even after the dust had settled. He was a tall, spindly kid who seemed to be even younger than the rest. In fact, Norman Rockwell could have used him for front page on the *Saturday Evening Post*. He was blond, had a well–chiseled face and, even in his tired condition, had a smile that barely showed. He must have played basketball and he played end on his high school team. I wanted to know him better—and, from that moment, for five years, our lives were entwined—in training for combat, for movement overseas and finally during two years of combat. It may not be a great story but it's our story.

This is also an attempt to share with the hometown folks something of what their sons and husbands went through to see that Japanese generals and dictators like Hitler didn't get control of these United States.

2
Getting an Assignment

There are hundreds of jobs to be done in an infantry division and someone is needed for each task. The Army processing center is just the place to find what you may be doing the rest of your life—at least, the rest of your army life. It is manned by "professionals" and is commanded by an even more specialized specialist.

You soon learn that the current needs of the division are the paramount factor. For instance, we have two recruits arrive who are world–famous pianists. We need one pianist for the division band so there is no immediate need for the second famous pianist. There is a great need for infantrymen. Therefore, the second pianist is assigned to one of the three infantry regiments. The processing center will try to fit you into your specialty, but you may end up fitting yourself into the specialty the army gives you.

***

Yesterday's arrivals at the railhead were still holding onto their barracks bags. They stood a little taller, patiently waiting for their assignment. Some had departed for their unit. I made my way through, talking to some about their hometown, to others about the train ride, the food, and to others, their families.

One kid was thirteen years old. He wasn't a young giant, but as I measured him with my eye, I thought he should lose some weight. He had a childish face and carried himself well. I asked him how he got through Selective Service; he went down to the induction center and volunteered. His folks were glad he was in the army, and he further informed me that he had already talked with twenty men who were fifteen and sixteen. I told him he could always find me at the division headquarter's chapel, or my sergeant could find me in a hurry.

***

When I went to Marfa, I wasn't assigned an assistant. I quickly decided that Command thought all a chaplain did was talk, he didn't need any assistance, but as I took on the post library which no one was using, they gave me a "dog–robber" quality fellow, and, to everyone's surprise, he soon learned to type, answer a phone, and began to clean up the library and my office. Then G–3 gave him a job as a private first class–and I never denied any individual the opportunity to advance. So I was assigned a succession of dog–robber–type privates that the captain and first sergeant had given up on—and each of them got better jobs. It always amazed me how men react to trust, responsibility and individual attention.

While still at Camp Gruber, things were different. We were allotted spaces for several assistants and I got Sgt. Arthur P. Van Iderstine in a most unusual way—or maybe not so unusual. The phone rang and a major from G–3 was calling. He had just interviewed a soldier he thought I could use. He was a conscientious objector. (A chaplain is a noncombatant. I had never seen any war but I visualized times in a battle where it might be a good idea to have a few guns around with men who could use them—and if push came to

14

shove I felt I could use one well enough.) So, to be fair, I told the major to send him down to the chapel. Soon a rawboned six–footer walked into my office. I asked him to sit down, and offered him a cup of coffee. I'm not sure he drank it, but I began to talk about his conscientious objections. He explained that he was against war, but he had been drafted anyway. I explained that most of us conscientiously objected to war but the Japs and the Germans didn't ask us if we wanted a war, I wasn't drafted, and I didn't have any children, but I didn't want them to grow up under the control of some dictator. I further explained that I could probably get him out of the army—since he was already in the system, it might take a while. He decided that he would like to work for a chaplain. He couldn't type but he was a graduate of Oberlin Conservatory of Music and wanted to be a professional organist—and long ago, I had decided that anyone who could play a piano or organ could learn to type in short order. Van became my right hand. He became my left; most of all he became my friend. We stayed together all during the war. He spent most of this time as a sergeant because this was the highest rank authorized for my office. He was a talented, efficient friend and associate. When he died a few years ago, I wept. Although fifty years have passed, I miss that magic we had together.

***

Back at the processing center, they were still calling out names over the loud speakers—and men were assigned a job they would be ordered to do. Many of these men had never been given a direct order in their life. Men often came to me and talked about the harshness of the army command system. In my mind, normally it wasn't harshness. It was directness. Personalities should not be involved. The general or the corporal has a job to do. He tells you to do your job—and there is not time for a seminar to discuss the pros and cons. The whole army system depends on acceptance of responsibility. If one soldier carries the tripod of a machine gun, another carries the ammunition. The other carries the barrel. The captain tells you to put the machine gun here and cover this area with fire. The guy with the barrel shows up, then comes the man with the tripod and they assemble the gun. If the guy with the ammunition has decided to rest or go to the bathroom (such as it is) and doesn't show with the ammunition, that part of the operation is delayed and in real combat, lots of men can get killed. In the army no one begs you to eat your Wheaties, but you can end up with a court martial if you fight the system.

***

Bars, leaves and stripes can give a lot of us a sense of superiority and an air of harshness. I was visiting a Jewish chaplain in his office and his secretary came to the door and said there was a man outside who wanted to see him. Thinking I was being a magnanimous senior chaplain, I motioned for her to send him in. A moment later a young kid showed up at the door, excusing himself for his hurry but he wanted to say good–bye to the young Jewish chaplain. The young fellow walked over to the chaplain and with tears in his voice said, "I'm being discharged in an hour but I want to thank you again for being so kind to me. You're the first person who's said a kind word to me since I left my mama."

A German dictator called his men his "dogs," but when his troops hiked through a forest, he posted guards on both sides of the forest road to assure his "dogs" didn't escape. I have known many dictators in my lifetime—of all ranks—but I have known many

16

others who appreciated their men, and when there was time, explained their aim, and they got cooperation in doing it.

***

At the processing center I was amazed at the inadequacies of our hometown induction efforts. I found one man with a crooked right arm. He kept trying to salute but he couldn't get his hand high enough. It took two months to get him out of the service.

Social and emotional injuries were always evident, but we had more difficulty dealing with them. I have never thought psychology was an exact science, but we do need people who can help the commander deal with fears, phobias and real mental sickness. I used to sit at an army headquarters between the army surgeon, the military police, Inspector General, and special services officer; I would remind them that none of them would have a job if our men didn't have social or mental problems. Since most of us have a few problems of our own, it's a good idea if I try to help and encourage others—not beat them down. For myself, I was determined to be a helper—not a hurter.

***

Luckily, I met my old friend Joe Rhoan again. He had just received his assignment to the 349th Infantry Regiment. He had no idea what he would be doing. He looked good this morning and wanted to talk. He told me about his twenty–two–hour train ride. Now he was waiting for a truck. No, he hadn't really been trained for anything. No, he didn't have any trouble doing what he was told. That's when he confessed he had a problem and he looked at his barracks bag. "This thing is killing me and I need to unload half of it."

He had grown up with an old maid aunt and she was so concerned about his well–being in the army that she insisted he bring with him what she thought were the basics of civilization. He said his barracks bag must weigh a hundred and fifty pounds. I agreed, because I had helped him get it on the truck. Now he was worried about storing the extras when he got to his barracks. What does a soldier do with twelve rolls of toilet paper, an electric iron, and electrically powered toothbrush (she was a great one for taking care of your teeth)? He had also brought one large quilt, a one—volume encyclopedia and an unabridged dictionary. Joe was literally hauling everything but the kitchen sink. He claimed he had moved the barracks bag at least a hundred times in the twenty–two hours of his train ride to Camp Gruber and the sixteen hours since he arrived. I promised he could stash any extras in one of the closets at the chapel, and I promised I'd drop by his company when I was in his regimental area. I also invited him to come by my chapel when he had time—but I didn't tell him that for the next six weeks he wouldn't have any time.

Every minute of every day would be controlled by his sergeant. He would be taught to march. (I reasoned that the army loved marching because it taught discipline and responsiveness.) The sergeant yells, "attention!" and every man, with tense body and focused mind awaits the next order. Whether he screams, "eyes right," "forward march," or "count off,"' every man in the formation responds or looks like a dope. When you march, you step in cadence. For the time being, every person in that particular command is under complete control of the commander...before long, when you are told to police the area, clean up the latrine, or peel potatoes, you go immediately to the task. The hope is that in combat you will respond the same way—even if your continued existence is problematic.

Battle Rattle

I had never marched in formation until I went to chaplain school. Several years after I became a chaplain, being a farmhand, a football player, and preacher hadn't given me the ability to keep in step: so I got up early and marched a few miles. I gave myself all the commands. I probably looked silly doing about face out in the boondocks. I learned, but I was glad that most times I stood with the commander in the reviewing stand and watched many thousands of good soldiers march by—and they were in step and in line—and I always got a thrill out of it. I did become a little more realistic six years later when I watched our troops parade down the streets of Gorizia, Italy. A beautiful, talented German girl we had liberated stood beside me as the troops passed by. I swelled with pride. She said, "Chaplain, I still miss the German army. They marched with such precision. Your men just march."

At first I was angry, but I knew she was speaking from her heart. I did remind her that we beat the hell out of them and that's why she could look out my window and express her opinion without fear of doing time in a stalag.

***

Not only do infantrymen learn how to march, they become conditioned to walk forty miles in a twenty-four–hour period carrying a lot of gear. My first army duty was the artillery. They didn't walk anywhere if they could help it. They had command cars, trucks to pull their howitzers, signal trucks, mess trucks, and maintenance vehicles. In my staff section, we had batteries and got us an electric razor. We could get a fresh shave before we came into a town. An infantry company, in those days, had a few jeeps and the mess truck. The supply truck and mess truck were usually

19

loaded with essentials—and that didn't include men. The infantry's job in World War II and before was that of a "foot soldier"—and many of these new recruits hadn't been asked to use their feet much. For six weeks, they would be force–fed in their qualification program, and for the next six months of their life, they would be taught to kill the enemy. They would be pushed like they had never been pushed in their lives—but some of us believed the stability of our world was at stake and we were willing to give a few years to this project—and thousands would literally give their lives.

I had a good home and I left! Right?

Next morning I visited the three regiments early. Now, all the training fields were filled with soldiers. Troop trains continued to arrive, and we were nearing our regular strength of fifteen thousand men. We had received a cadre of experienced soldiers from another division, and they were already at work. Men had been assigned to squads and platoons, and the task of converting civilians into soldiers had begun in earnest. Hundreds of new recruits were being herded into barely recognizable formations over every square foot of huge training fields.

The first group of recruits marched by in a typical first–time sort of order. They were out of step most of the time. Their lines were sloppy, but they were no longer the tired troops of yesterday. Youth had triumphed again. They wore clean fatigues. Somewhere they had had their long hair sheared. Their caps fit fairly well, and they had polished their boots. They had been up most of the night, and the few hours of sleep did wonders for them, but that didn't help them perform close order drill. Ears were not accustomed to the shrill, unintelligible commands of their drillmasters. Mind and feet were not synchronized, nor was the nervous system grooved to respond in sufficient time to avert catastrophe to the army's prized sense of order.

***

Few civilians and relatively few military men have bothered to understand the trauma of recruit training where all men are adjusted to fit the army's procrustean standard. (In this bed, if you are too long you get chopped off to fit—if you are too short you are stretched until you fit the bed.) This phase of training is designed to make disciplined, orderly, obedient soldiers out of raw civilians, but, to be made into a soldier in eight weeks requires a human being to reform much of his thought process, change much of his concept of his own relationship to authority, and be fitted into a model of man that was unknown and inconceivable to him when he raised his right hand at the induction center and swore to uphold and protect the United States from all enemies, foreign and domestic. His routine sense of personal freedom and rights of the individual must be tailored to "the army way." In many ways, the recruit is taught to act like a robot. He must learn all about weapons; some are taught to assemble their personal weapon blindfolded. He learns, in the field to sleep with his rifle; he rolls his socks in a certain way and lines his personal items up in a personal way for inspection. (I had a son in the Air Force Academy that lined up his socks in his footlocker for inspection and he kept that line–up ready at all times—to such an extent he didn't change socks for six weeks. He was so busy he couldn't go to the PX to purchase extras—and I smile, as I think of the inspector admiring his fine display in the foot locker, and not smelling my son's awful feet.)

21

Further, the recruit must learn the procedures in dealing with different levels of authority. He treats the corporal one way; he deals with the sergeant in another. The lieutenant becomes superman and his captain becomes a super superman. He may comprehend later that there are even higher ranks, but these are the limits of his recruit world.

***

There is no privacy for a private. He waits in a line with other naked men. He has to wait for a medical corpsman or a doctor to punch him in the scrotum, rectum, and penis; they look into his eyes, ears, and throat—all with less concern that they would examine an old coin. Both arms are loaded with immunization shots. In preparing to go overseas, officers and enlisted men marched through a gauntlet where they were given six shots—three in each arm. He becomes a serial number and is told to wear his dog tags to the latrine, bed, and training. He finds commodes lined up like thrones and urination and defecation become a public affair.

***

The long–time result of a close order drill is a mystery to anyone not acquainted with rote learning and mental reinforcement. Men can be marched in squads, platoons, companies, battalions, regiments, divisions, corps and armies, but each man is taught to respond to the command 'tenshut' to such an extent that I have imagined that if in the dead of night someone yelled 'tenshut', a disciplined soldier would awake in the darkness, and jump to attention at the side of his bed. They give the recruit orders like "present–arms" or "forward–march," and he immediately learns to interpret and execute the command. The soldier is marched and marched days and weeks till he reacts automatically. I was in the army three years before I interpreted the command "right–a black." When I went to chaplain school I got hold of a training manual and found that the drill sergeant was yelling "right–oblique."

***

I came to the 349th regimental training area and hundreds of recruits were bringing down on themselves the impatient wrath of training sergeants who had little pity for slow learners. My favorite trainer was Sergeant Kovechni—I heard him screaming, "Halt," with his wonderful Polish accent. He was a good professional soldier who had become overburdened with the slow progress of his troops, and even though he yelled, "Halt," again, half of his contingent kept on marching. One by one they recognized something was awry and straggled to a stop. The burly old sergeant placed his hands on his head and suffered. He did not curse at anyone as I expected. He just became more visibly apoplectic as he marched around and around in tight circles before them. The soldiers couldn't decide if this display was comedy or tragedy, but no one laughed. Finally, the old sergeant got himself under control and stood there looking at them as if three days ago these men were ordering poached eggs on toast and complaining if their mother or wife had overcooked the bacon.

Finally, he gathered his chicks together; got them formed in lines; had them link their arms together with the man on his right. With a withering look and roaring like a lion, he threatened any man who broke ranks with, "A month in the kitchen doing KP." Again, he warned the rear ranks to keep up with the rank in front. His voice kept getting higher and higher until he was shouting commands in Polish with a southern accent. And by the time he ordered them to, "Forward, march," the formation disintegrated. Men were scurrying to get back into ranks but a frustrated but wiser lieutenant yelled, "At ease!" and then gave them a ten–minute break.

For soldiers who had not learned to march, they had quickly learned to take full advantage of a rest break. I began moving toward Sergeant Kovechni, and he began apologizing for his men. I assured him that in a few days, with his instruction, they would get the hang of close order drill.

**

One of the casualties of the marching catastrophe was Joe Rhoan. He had stationed himself about twenty feet away from Sergeant Kovechni. From his vantage point, he managed his wry smile as I walked toward him. He and six other fellow sufferers were wrestling with the situation. They assured me that they had a good night's sleep, a nice breakfast, and Joe informed me he had dumped his surplus equipment into the trash barrel. I told them that Sergeant Kovechi knew his business and I knew they would be much improved in a few days. I also suggested they keep trying—for it would take lots of effort to get the mind and the body and the feet to cooperate with the sergeant's commands. Thinking about and practicing a bit as I walked to chow had helped me. The same would help them. I did believe they would react in split seconds to Sergeant Kovechni. They might even begin to enjoy marching as a unit.

The sergeant called them to return to their formation. They formed up and he called them to attention and they looked pretty good. He commanded them, "Forward, march,"—and they did—and Sergeant Kovechni threw me a salute—and I threw him one back. We both knew that each day of the drill would become easier, smoother and more spontaneous. These recruits were in the throes of a most difficult lesson. When you get a command in the army you are expected to react not only properly, but instantaneously.

3

Thou Shalt Kill

The next time I saw Joe Rhoan, he was looking down the barrel of an army rifle. He was stretched out on his stomach with the rifle stock cramped into his right shoulder. A sergeant knelt over him telling him when and how to breathe—and how to squeeze the trigger. The target came rising out of the pits like some stark giant and Joe squeezed his rounds off until the clip was empty. He rolled over rather confidently and quietly waited with the sling still on his arm—but it was easy to tell he was not worried about his score. The marker began marking the score. Joe was a qualified Sharp Shooter, entitled to wear his first badge—one among many he collected within the years we were to know each other.

This time he rose, smiled, and walked over to where I stood. I congratulated him on his fine shooting. He accepted my praise, but didn't seem as jubilant as I would have been. He did talk easily about close–order drill and laughed out loud when he recalled the catastrophes of his first few days of service.

"Even Sergeant Kovechni is bragging about our platoon," he said. "We can even do several to–the–rear marches without falling apart," But his mood changed quickly and in an undertone, as if afraid some bystander might hear, he asked, "Chaplain, will you be in your office tonight?"

"Sure, Joe, I'll be looking for you when you finish chow." I nodded good–bye just in time to be attracted to a commotion further down the firing line.

A heavyset kid with bad teeth had gone berserk. He had a mouth full of rotten teeth and hadn't been in the army long enough to get them fixed up—and it looked like his stay would be too short–lived for much free dentistry. The sergeant had finally coaxed him into the prone position, had instructed him on the firing procedure—but when the reluctant novice pulled the trigger and the rifle bucked in his arms and the explosion tore at his ears, he threw down the rifle, jumped up from the firing line, and looked as if he were heading right into the line of fire of the shooter next to him. He dodged back behind the line of fellows waiting their turn to test their shooting prowess.

He stood there yelling, weeping, frothing, and grabbing his chest as if he were bordering on a heart attack—and the old army sergeant who had been patiently instructing him stood open–mouthed, watching all these gyrations as if it were beyond his ken or imagination for anyone to produce all this emotional imbalance over one little rifle shot.

I walked over to this Brooklyn One–Man Hurricane and said, "I am a chaplain. What's all this about?" I had counted on a good Roman Catholic exposure to the local priest for I felt this man had been one of Brooklyn's priestly problems. Sure enough, the view of the crosses on the collar of my uniform and the positive statement brought distinct relaxation.

He began protesting in a loud voice, obviously for the Rifle Instructor's ear, as well as mine. "Father, I just can't stand loud noises—and that rifle is impossible."

(I got used to being called Father by the Catholics and I'm sure the chaplain priests eventually got used to some Texas Baptist calling them Brother or Reverend.)

He tried to light a cigarette and he couldn't connect the flaming match to the end of it. I took the match and lighted his smoke and finally got him into conversation. He kept telling me he had always been afraid of rifles, but he was slowly settling down to his own sort of normalcy.

We talked about his home, his church, and the school he hadn't managed to attend very much. It was plain he didn't have many assets that usually belonged to soldiers. He had little concept of patriotism. He had no family. He had courted a few girls, but had never been serious about any of them. He was a plain bumbler and, up until he had been drafted, he got through life by feigning irresponsibility. He had thrown away every decent job much like he had thrown away his rifle. We talked till chow time.

I didn't see him again for three weeks. I was going into the Orderly Room early one morning and he came rushing over to me waving is discharge papers. He was on his way home. He was happy to return to his old life and we were happy to see him go.

4

Life in an Army Chapel

Division Headquarters Chapel was like hundreds of others built across the United States: simple in architecture, utilitarian in design, and authorized by Congress to become the religious and spiritual center of that particular military community. Catholic, Protestant, and Jewish services were conducted regularly. There were offices for one, two, or three chaplains. Like the New England Town Meeting House, the chapel became a center for men who wanted a neutral area in which to congregate, for men who wanted to worship, and men who needed to confide to a religious leader their sins, their hurts, and their beefs.

There have been those who think a chaplain should not have officer status. Regardless of my rank, I always felt I was the one man in the military complex that could cross the chasm between the Enlisted and the Officer groups at will. I felt comfortable lying under a tree shooting the breeze with a private and a sergeant or eating a meal with the highest–ranking general. I was a professional, trained to do my job within my religious principles.

I knew more about my job than any man in my command. I stood for morality in battle. I preached the inherent need of men to have a spiritual foundation

31

and fountain in their life. I was there to love and help soldiers—whether they were privates or Five–Star generals. I always had a sneaking suspicion that some people wearing stars on this earth may be lucky enough to do KP in eternity. I had to exist within the military environment but my first priority was the human soul. Taxpayers paid me to represent the spiritual side of human life within the high–walled autocracy of the military system.

I had converted one of the front rooms of my chapel into a sort of church parlor. Women from the First Baptist Church in Muskogee, Oklahoma kept the cookie jar filled, and there were comfortable chairs for sitting and a refreshing drink was available. Several soldiers had come by and discussed the day's activities at the rifle range. Laugher was uproarious as one of the ever–present comedians gave his impression of some of the events of the day.

Joe Rhoan came to the door and stood there as the conversation was batted from one corner of the room to the other. He did not add anything so I worked my way to the doorway and out into the vestibule. I motioned for him to come with me through the chapel to my office.

I sensed that Joe was deeply troubled about something, so I pulled the door closed and we sat down. He gnawed his lower lip for a few seconds and then the dam burst.

"Chaplain, I'm afraid I'm not cut out for soldiering. I didn't mind Sergeant Kovechni and the marching. I can see some good in calisthenics, policing the area, cleaning the barracks—I didn't mind when the Sergeant threw us a rifle and began teaching us to assemble and disassemble it. I learned every part. I could break it down in seconds, but I began to feel bad when they gave me a bayonet and told me to put

32

it on the gun. One of the corporals demonstrated how you jammed the bayonet into a man and how it was yanked out so it would be ready again for immediate use. He said, 'When you push the bayonet into a man's chest, there is a thud like a base drum being hit. When you pull it out, there may be a gurgle.' To make the demonstration better, the corporal, at his own expense, brought a ripe watermelon and split it with the bayonet. He reached in, took the heart out, and began to eat the red meat. For the first time since I got here, I became sick. I suddenly realized what I was drafted for; I am being taught to kill people—and I'm not sure I can do it."

Joe had the picture and I would be the last to tell him he had missed the point. The Army is designed to defeat the enemy—and this means human beings. "The battle is the pay off," we had been told time and time again. Men, who had adventurously killed a few sparrows, or stepped on a half dozen caterpillars in a whole lifetime, were now being trained to effectively destroy enemy battalions; and the enemy was people: men, married to women; fathers of children; young men filled with vitality, and delivered into the army by their own neighbors on the Selective Service Board. The enemy loved, hurt, wept, dreamed like each of us—and Joe was faced with the realization of the nature of his job.

"Joe," I said, "you have learned a great deal the last few days. You have come to see the job of the soldier as it really is, but look at it in a broader perspective. Just like the sheriff back in your hometown has been deputized to protect the bank and the citizens, you have been deputized to deal with this country's enemies. They are ready to take over one of our allies. They have already destroyed many countries and taken away the freedom of millions of people. I sincerely feel they would take over our country if they got a chance. They would take over our wives and our children. They would steal our gold and our industry. I think we have a right to protect these things. I would not be foolish enough to tell you that the enemy doesn't feel the same way—but I still have to do what I feel is right. No war is altogether good, but war now may be better than something else later on."

I went on to tell Joe that I believed the Old Testament Commandment usually translated, "Thou shalt not kill," would be better translated, "Thou shall not commit murder." I reminded him that the same Moses who brought down the commandments from the mountain found the Children of Israel dancing around the Gold Calf. I read the Bible to him where Moses was so incensed that he threw down the stone tablets and broke them. He then called for those men who were still on the Lord's side and led them forth to slay the idolaters with swords. I quoted from the Bible, "And there fell of the people that day about three thousand men."

There was no doubt in my mind that Moses did not feel that God precluded law and order. He also led the Israelites into battle until his death. Jesus healed the Centurion's daughter. He could have told the Centurion he would have to give up the soldier's profession before he could do anything for him. "No, I believe that, for the time being, we must defend our country against its enemies—and Joe—that means you and every other able–bodied American—who can stand the brunt of war."

Joe listened carefully for he knew I was speaking to his feelings. He could not buy all that I was saying because he had not thought along these lines. He thanked me for talking with him and headed back to his barracks.

Joe and millions like him were in my thoughts as I worked back in my office. Few people understand the trauma that goes into the making of a soldier. We live in a land that worships zest and vitality and life. We fear death. We advertise soap, cars, books with vivacious youngsters and well–preserved and good–looking men and women. We spend more time and money saving a life than any nation in the world.

Suddenly, one of our better young men is drafted into the military or perhaps he volunteers. He's immediately told that his job is killing. The killers he has known have been thugs in the news or in the artificial situation of the movies, but he is now being trained with a seriousness and lethality that shocks his innermost emotions and sensibilities.

I started for the troop area. As I walked through the chapel, a loud groaning sound came from the rest room near the front door. Lying on the floor in the midst of a pool of blood was a soldier. I rushed to the phone, called an ambulance, and hurried back to the fellow. He had cut his wrist with a razor blade (not very deeply), and had tried to let the blood run into the commode. When he fainted, he had fallen to the floor. It was then that I had heard his groaning.

Using my thumb to stop the bleeding, I stretched him out on the chapel rug and held him until the ambulance came. I rode with him to the hospital and sat waiting while they repaired his razor incisions. One–and–a–half hours later, he was taken to a ward. I stayed with him until he came out from the anesthetic, and let him know help was available.

The patient was older than the other soldiers in the outfit. He had been drafted at a very critical time in his life. He had finally concluded he could not become a soldier so he was taking the only way out he knew.

He had wanted to come into the Army. He loved being with the young men in his outfit.

Speaking in an undertone that could not be heard by the patient in the next bed, his disillusionment began to surface. "When I was too tired in the morning to get going, the younger guys jumped out of bed when the Sergeant started yelling. They got shaved and dressed and then stood in the old morning Reveille Formation, listening patiently to the long–drawn–out dreary announcements and roll call. Me, I was damned sick of twenty–year–old corporals and twenty–one–year–old lieutenants playing soldier. It goes to the place where it was no longer a game and the straw that broke the camel's back came last night. We have an eighteen–year–old clown in our outfit that still has not learned to obey orders. After the officer had gone home the sergeant came in and got him and took him out on the parade ground. He made the kid push a peanut across the parade ground and back with his nose. The kid finished the peanut rolling task, stood calmly, and then floored the unsuspecting NonCom with a fast right to the jaw.

"The guy hit the ground, sat up on his buttocks, thought for a second, and then he calmly arose and beat hell out of the kid. Both of them were a bloody mess when they came into the latrine and got cleaned up. By the time they had showered and used a bottle of Mercurochrome, they were laughing and had planned to tell the lieutenant that they had tripped over each other coming downstairs—and both of them lived on the first floor of the barracks.

"I had heard about the discipline of the First Sergeants in the Old Army. I had witnessed the forced clean–up of a mountaineer kid who wouldn't take a bath. He smelled like a pig and the First Sergeant got a heavy bristle brush normally used for cleaning the floors, a bar of lye soap and the kid. They both disappeared into the shower stall and the kid came out clean and rubbed raw. Nobody ever had to tell him to take a bath again.

"In fact most of the sergeants in this outfit are hard–working mature disciplinarians, but last night I got a bellyful. I cried in my sleep and woke feeling like the wrath of God.

"I tried to get through breakfast—and I would have made it—but there was an Orthodox Jewish kid in front of me. He's had a hell of a time eating. He asked the cook for poached eggs. The cook knew the kid's problem with food that wasn't kosher, but he was too damned lazy to care. He put the eggs in a bowl and made like he was pouring hot water over them, but turned and dropped the eggs in a puddle of bacon grease. The kid took some toast and coffee and went into the Mess, but I began yelling and cursing the damn' cook. I wanted to kill him.

"Guys from my company grabbed me and took me out into the fresh air. I told them I was okay, but wandered around for two hours. I didn't know where to go. In fact, there is no place for a soldier to go once he has raised his right hand and stepped forward—except where he is told to go. I walked over to the chapel and sat for a while. I heard your typewriter, but I just didn't care anymore. I started to walk out but felt the pack of razor blades I had placed in my pocket. It seemed like the only way out. I walked into the restroom and cut my wrist. I guess I didn't have the guts to cut it deeper but the blood poured out and I didn't want to mess up the chapel. I just stood there and bled into the commode—and that's the last thing I remember till I woke up here."

Assuring the patient that there was help somewhere for him in this vast military mass production system of Commanders, Doctors, Chaplains, and Adjutant Generals, I promised to drop by tomorrow at two o'clock. I was in better luck than I could have imagined for when I arrived at the Officers Mess, the Commanding General and the Division Surgeon were also eating late. I told them about my conversation. The surgeon suggested that I take the matter up with one of his staff in the morning. It sounded to him like "a case of inability to adjust."

I finally got to bed, tired out, but reassured for the first time —in my military corner—that when the time came to stop this big production wheel and extricate an individual with some special need, the machine could be halted for a brief second. I nestled into the cover feeling sort of like Joshua felt when he learned that he could stop the sun in its path when he needed more daylight to win a battle.

I never forgot the lessons learned before I said, "good–bye," to this potential suicide. I knew few commanders who did not want what was best for the unit they commanded. When I could justify changes or decisions that improved the unit I would make them. I received top–level support. I became a recognized staff officer—not just one assigned a certain task—but one who was a team player and brought fairness, loyalty and kindness to those problems that can undermine the spirit of the troops.

5

Selective Service in Charge

The following Friday, I spent about two hours on the drill fields. I was now proud of the fine formations, the spirited marching, the general physical health, and the enthusiasm of the soldiers. Sergeants and trainees were really developing a team.

I struck out for the chapel and fell in step with one of the lieutenants striding along in the same direction. He was from Kansas, had received a Thomason Act commission, and was a bright, promising young man. He wanted to get married to a childhood sweetheart before he went overseas. He had been an all All–Conference basketball player, but in this hectic period, he couldn't even play tennis. He didn't like Camp Gruber, Oklahoma (too far from anything) but he didn't mind the weather. "Weather is worse back in Kansas," he said.

As the lieutenant split off to the Orderly Room, and we were sort of exchanging good–byes, a soldier came by and shocked us both with a left-handed salute. The lieutenant, in normal military fashion, stopped the soldier and began to chew him out, "You may be left handed, but we get ambidextrous enough in this outfit to salute with our right hand."

He glanced at the soldier's right hand, and it was actually withered and deformed. He couldn't raise his right hand to his brow without bending his head downward.

This kid had been drafted, inducted, and shipped six hundred miles to division training for actual combat. Again, I headed for the Surgeon's office, with the soldier in tow. Thousands of dollars later—and probably one pension—the soldier was discharged and on his way home.

Wherever I went, soldiers bitched about the army. They felt the Army had personally come to their home and dragged them out and forced them into training. One of my tasks was to give them the facts. Unless they had volunteered, their own neighbors, using rules given to them by the National Selective Service Commission, had named them for induction. They had been brought into the Army by the law of the land. The Army's job is to make soldiers out of the men sent to them by the Selective Service Boards across the nation. In a real sense the Draft is a local affair with ground rules that come out of a local interpretation of national guidelines.

I always had great sympathy for the Selective Service Board. I could imagine farmers, merchants, grandmothers, and various other people in the United Sates coming directly or indirectly to the Selective Service Board to justify their son, husband or friend of a friend being deferred. No father in his right mind sends his son off to war and no mother gives her permission to his becoming a soldier without a great deal of reservation.

But, the one situation in which I always had the greatest interest and which I sympathized with the Selective Service Board the most was in the matter of conscientious objection. I never knew what a conscientious objector was. I never could understand the basis on which men were judged to be conscientious in their objection to war. I knew some men who conscientiously objected to one war and did not object to another war. I had traveled nearly every avenue that conscientious objectors can travel. I found that most of them who called themselves conscientious objectors, objected because their parents were objectors. Some of them belonged to churches that emphasized conscientious objection to all combat. Many were willing to serve in a non–combatant position and would spend the war doing some of the bravest things that man could ever do.

Roman Catholics, at this particular time, could bring themselves to accept a "just" war, but I found that most Protestants were basically pacifistic. They hated war. They felt that war was sinful. They honestly considered that their participation in war was against their religious principles and yet most of them then went on to war, and did a good job.

One day an officer told me, "Chaplain, when the war is over, I am going to get myself straightened out with God, and then I am going to live a Christian life."

I asked him what he meant by "straightened out."

He replied, "No man can fight a war and do what Christ taught him to do."

I reminded him that as a Chaplain, I was an accomplice to this fact and that I felt that I was bringing religious ministry to men who had been deputized by their Nation to go out and destroy an enemy, an enemy who was threatening us.

One day I had a call from one of my company commanders, asking me to talk with one of his soldiers who claimed to be a conscientious objector. Now, mind you, there were sufficient guidelines so that any man who was a conscientious objector should have applied to the local Selective Service Board before his induction notice and he could have been deferred because of his status. He might also have been labeled as a conscientious objector who could not bear arms. On that basis, we could have placed him in a medical unit or some other unit where he would not have had to carry a rifle. But many men didn't know how to apply to the Selective Service Board. They didn't realize the nature of their military obligation until they got into the training situation. Bayonet training, rifle fire, the very attitude of some of the officers as they spoke to the men, made them realize that, really, the grisly part of military life was killing—killing other human beings. And, this was repulsive to men who have lived in peace with their fellow men, who envisioned a life of comfort, a good home, sturdy children, and a fine wife. It was repulsive to their dream for the future.

At any rate, this young man came into my office, and I asked him why he hadn't gone to the Selective Service Board. He told me he didn't know that he was supposed to do that. I reminded him that ignorance of the law was no excuse and then we began to talk in our own religious competence. We discussed the Old Testament. I told him about my conference with Joe Rhoan, though I didn't mention Joe by name, and reminded him that many men in this outfit were in similar position in their thinking to him.

In fact, I felt that the majority of men feel that war is "sinful," and yet there is nothing in the Old Testament that would even countenance conscientious objection to war. War was either holy or it was not holy. Moses could lead his men into combat, Joshua led his soldiers into war, David and most of the rest of the Jewish leaders were combat people, and they gloried in their military victories.

Again, he brought up the same idea as Joe Rhoan. The scripture says, "Thou shalt not kill." I reminded him that the same Moses who brought down the law, "Thou shalt not kill," slew thousands of his own men with a sword when he came down from the holy mountain and found them dancing around the golden calf. Then we went to the New Testament—Jesus taught that if a man strike thee on one cheek, thou shalt turn the other. He told us that we should agree with our enemies, and that we should love our enemies.

In fact, the New Testament teaches us that we should live peaceably with all men if it is at all possible.

But I reminded him that at the end of 100 A.D., there were many Christians in the armed forces and that by 330 A.D., Constantine had become a Christian and became the greatest Christian general of all Europe. Peter did not hesitate to take a sword and chop off one of the Roman soldier's ears after all the teaching and the time he had been with Jesus. I encouraged him to go on and train and to further discuss the thing, because he wasn't going to be called on to kill anyone for quite a while. And as he talked with other men, and as he worked with other men, if he really came to the place where he felt that God was going to condemn him to eternal hell for killing somebody, or if he felt that any kind of bearing arms was inconsistent with his religious beliefs, in a way this meant to me that he no longer could have the peace that comes with having a good policeman circling his block and protecting him again potential robbers. To me, a good conscientious objector would not lift a finger against somebody stealing from him, killing him, raping his wife, or doing anything. He would use no means of force, neither a clenched fist, nor a baseball bat, nor a rifle, or a .45 pistol to protect himself.

The young man thought this over, and then with confidence in me (which scared me a bit), he said, "Chaplain, I'll go back and do the training. I'll think about it and pray about it. And if I find that I cannot bear arms, I'll come and let you know. My biggest problem is what if I come to the conclusion that I really cannot serve in the military because of my religious convictions?"

I smiled and told him, "Well, this is one bridge we will have to cross later. You're in now. You could have stayed out originally. But I'll give you all the help I can when the time comes."

Later on, the Provost Marshall called and gave me another problem. "We have," he said, "a man in the stockade we want you to talk with." They soon brought this young fellow to my office. He was dressed in prison fatigues. I asked him what he had done, and he claimed he was a conscientious objector, and the army was mistreating him. He had been in solitary on bread and water for about two weeks. Now, he had threatened that he would not even eat the bread or drink the water and would starve to death. Again, he was a county lad. His family had been conscientious objectors in World War I. He had been taught that war was wrong, but he had thought when he got down to the induction station he could talk "to those people," and they would send him back home. He didn't realize that by the time he got to the induction station, the mass production cycle was in full swing. And "those people" did not decide or undecide. Their job was to induct and inducted he was. He was brought right into the military service.

He kept talking to people all along the line, saying, "How do I get off this thing?" And he found that this treadmill only went one way and that was forward. Finally, when he got to the outfit, he decided to take his stand. He talked with his platoon sergeant. He talked with the company commander. He talked with his chaplain and everybody threw up their hands and said there was nothing that could be done. His only alternative, as he saw it, was to tell his sergeant that he was not going to take part in any military training. Before he knew it, he was put in military prison. His trial had not come up. In fact, they didn't quite know what to do with him. That's why they had sent him to me, to see if I could make some recommendations.

This young fellow had the same basic objections as all conscientious objectors, but in his mind, he could not bear arms. He could not kill anybody, in spite of the fact that the attacker was the enemy, that the attacker was trying to kill him, or in spite of any other situation I could raise. He had finally decided that he would die of starvation by his own hand before he would go along any further with military training.

I asked him did he have any objection to helping people who had to bear arms, was he willing to serve in the medical battalion?

"Oh, yes, that would be fine," he said. He just didn't want to take up a rifle and kill anybody. I reminded him, too, that in the Geneva Conventions, he was obligated, or at least had a right to protect his patients; that might mean someday, if he were left alone behind the lines with some wounded men, he might be called on to try to protect these patients. He still couldn't kill; he couldn't fire rifles or any other firearms under these circumstances. So again, using very fine staff cooperation, we transferred this young fellow to the medical battalion, and he was trained to work in an operating room and in medical wards.

Through the years, I met these men time and time again. I met men in the heat of combat, men who had tested themselves, and it always worried me. I sympathize with the Selective Service Board, because I feel that ninety percent of all men are basically against war. They are against it in the depths of their hearts, their minds and their bodies. Most of them are more conscientiously objecting than many of the clergymen. Clergymen, in the American Revolutionary War, were some of the greatest generals and some of the most active line officers that George Washington had. Many of them continued as clergymen, but led troops. Many of them became chaplains in the armed forces and served their country. Clergymen are still some of the most vigorous leaders in the support of their country in military endeavors.

But I still worry about the mass of men, who really haven't thought about the cost of war, or who don't know what to do in case they are called to war. They go, they raise their right hand, they serve, and many of them kill, with a gnawing feeling underneath that this thing should not have taken place.

Gen. S.L.A. Marshall, in evaluation of World War II, after it was over, and in consideration of the efforts of soldiers in the wars of Europe and Asia in the past one hundred years, contends that only twenty–five percent of the soldiers ever, under any circumstance, fire their weapons; generals wonder why.

Seldom do we take the time to ask ourselves if this war has enough moral consequences for us to involve our people. We fight for oil, we fight for rubber, we fight for land. But seldom do we ask ourselves, "Is this war moral or immoral?" I believe some wars are moral, but certainly many wars should never have been fought.

6
Individual Training

Usually training of recruits is done wholesale. The basic unit is a squad of eight to twelve men and the total number of men to be trained is subdivided into effective training units. At one time a military training center may be training hundreds or thousands of squads.

Since my particular outfit was a division being trained for combat, it had a training cadre that had been taught how to train other soldiers. The rest of the division was made up of thousands of Selectees that arrived fresh from urban and rural U.S. at a ratio of approximately one man with experience to ten who had none; the business of converting raw civilians into trained combatants took place at a feverish rate.

Our Commanding General, commanding this infantry division, was a former Coast Artilleryman and a graduate of the Naval Academy. He was intense, enthusiastic, and knew how to command. He had the first Selective Service Division to be put together and he meant for it to be the best–trained outfit that ever launched an attack. This first phase of Individual Training was to be thorough and effective, and it was. Gen. John R. Sloan was not called (to his back) "Johnny Eager" for nothing. He was everywhere at all hours of the day and night.

Individual Training insures that the Individual Infantry Soldier knows everything about everything he is supposed to use. His rifle and bayonet is his basic weapon, and whether he plays in the band, operates a mimeograph in Division Headquarters, or cooks in the General's Mess, he must be prepared to do combat duty. He learns about personal sanitation. In combat a man can be floored by dysentery as completely as he can be floored by a bullet. Bad feet reduce a man's effectiveness and an infantryman uses his feet as basic transportation.

Men were encouraged to go to church. They received psychological, sociological and character conditioning, but the first eight weeks are mainly marching, physical training, shooting, bayoneting, and cleaning clothes.

We had a physical conditioning course that helped develop the sort of physical dexterity some officers conceived might be needed in any combat condition though few men ever needed all the dexterities this one course envisioned. There were pull–ups, solid wooden fences to scale, ropes to climb, mazes to run through, ditches to jump (some with water), Tarzan swings, tortuous obstacles to wriggle through, narrow ledges to traverse—and all to be done at break–neck speed.

I caught Joe Rhoan as his outfit had stripped to the waist for morning calisthenics. The Sergeant, giving orders in a concise and staccato series of burps, ran through the programmed exercises with precision. The troops were in good condition and the lieutenant who was observing only had to give gentle reminders to the few men who were lagging a bit. I smiled at the improvement the men were making, for only a few weeks ago they would have fallen over if they had been exposed to this much physical exertion.

Then came their trip through, over, and around the obstacle course. To my surprise, the lieutenant and the sergeant both took off with the herd. The first fifty yards was a dead run into the face of an eight foot wall. For the larger men, the trick was to reach over the top of the wall for a good handhold and then to pull the body over with one motion. For a small man, the top of the wall was one huge jump and grab. All but two men made it over the wall on the first try. The knotted rope climb was more difficult. A slim fellow like Joe Rhoan could reach up on the rope with his hands and pull his taut body to the top by placing one hand above the other and lifting. A bigger man like me had to use feet and hands and legs and struggle to the top. There was hardly enough strength to pull the body over to the pole ladder and climb furiously down. Joe could run through the maze of boxes with the grace of a ballet dancer, but some men stumbled and fell. Crawling under the barbed wire required patience.

One man was caught in the barbs and a fellow soldier got him loose and everyone proceeded through the various obstacles at break–neck speed. I left Joe, Sergeant Kovechni, and the lieutenant led the pace—but Kovechni was straining to keep up with the lieutenant.

Some individuals just don't train easily. The post office crew in our Headquarters Company mainly represented the fair environs of the Bronx, and what a group of representatives they were. I loved the bunch of them—but I still shudder at their island of independence within that ocean of authority.

This particular morning was gas mask drill and training. The entire Headquarters Company was drawn in full array and this was a sight to behold. These fellows were the cream of the military crop—for the particular purposes for which they had been chosen. They were the best educated and best trained of the fifteen thousand men we had received. In a sense, they were the prima donnas of our Division—but they proved to be the most effective administrative group I ever saw.

They were lined up, but the procedure was stalled. Soldiers stood on one foot and then the other. Sergeants were moving rather swiftly for Headquarters' sergeants. Officers were chafing at their bits. This was to be a one–hundred–percent affair—and then there appeared at the door of one of the barracks one of the biggest representatives of the postal contingent. Every other soldier had his gas mask properly strapped to his side—but out came our hero—with four hundred men waiting—bearing in his arms the original fully–sealed cardboard carton. While everyone watched, he carefully opened the carton, took the gas mask and canvas cover out of the cellophane, properly placed it in the proper order, strapped it to his side and walked nonchalantly over to the post office contingent and calmly awaited the order to come to attention and prepare for gas mask inspection.

The momentous inspection began—fifteen minutes late.

This same character provided me the funniest story I ever heard in the war. We had been in combat many months and this postal crew had functioned magnificently. They knew enough about postal regulations and procedures to get salami from home. I tasted my first anchovies in their tent. There was always a new store of delicacies to destroy the taste of Spam and mutton.

In fact, nightly, I visited them just to find out what was new. They had the most delightful stories, the gayest banter, and a most unusual sort of camaraderie; all this in the midst of war, mud, and loneliness. I got a boost from just being present, but this one night the place was filled with an unusual vocal pandemonium.

The contingent was quartered in one room of a large Italian barn. A Liberty ship convoy had arrived at a neighboring port with the mail and on the previous day, the vans of mail for the division had been dumped into the barn in a stack fifteen feet high for sorting and delivery. (Unit mailmen were always stopping by to see the division postal crew and I had a division–wide intelligence system at a constant peak of operational efficiency. They knew how the attacks were going, what commander was having trouble, the rate of casualties. Just name it and they knew it.)

Our division had an Adjutant General, a professional soldier and a West Pointer, who had been exposed to a full broadside of Oriental Theosophy on one of his tours in Hawaii. He believed in a sort of Pantheism. It was a sort of "God is in everything" approach. He believed in the divinity of all life. He wouldn't kill a snake on Louisiana maneuvers; he wouldn't use fly spray to kill flies. He also had some unusual ideas about physical matter. He believed all of life was reincarnated and he couldn't destroy a mosquito with Flit for fear he was bombing one of his ancestors.

The colonel, by thought transport and mental projection could do an unusual gymnastic, at least for most of us. He could go home at night. Since we were buried in snow in the mountains south of Bologna, and since his home was somewhere in the Middle Western part of the United States, going home at night was a neat trick. In fact, if the colonel showed up at work a few minutes late in the morning, some quick–witted sergeant would calmly announce, "I guess the colonel got snowed in at Pittsburgh last night." Everyone laughed—that is, till the colonel appeared.

But there was one other philosophical phobia that didn't bring laughter. The colonel believed that a man must live his life in conformity to magnetic physical forces—and that, translated into dormitory terminology, meant he had to sleep with his feet headed west and his head headed east—in line with the rays and pull of the sun. So when we moved into a new bivouac—and sometimes this was in over three feet of snow, his sleeping trailer had to be headed right. More than one time, he got to his trailer at ten or eleven o'clock at night and got his trusty compass to see if he were going to recline in the right direction—and found he was fifteen degrees off the right track. He rang the sergeant major. The sergeant major rang the ground crew (usually those fellows who ran mimeograph machines or typewriters during the day), and the ground crew got dressed and went out into the Alpine freeze and set the colonel's trailer exactly right.

I know all this because they complained a wee bit to the Chaplain—and in true Army Brass tradition, I advised them to be grateful the colonel didn't have worse vices.

But the colonel, though he had been shunted from the main tactical responsibility to an administrative sideline, had one main aim in his combat life and that was to see that the mail got through to the fighting troops. When he heard about the deliveries of these latest tons of mail, he came down to see that it was sent forward to the front at full speed. But life was to offer one of those rough days all men face.

The Postal Crew had spent four frantic hours unloading the tons of mail from the truck vans that delivered the sacks from Leghorn Port one hundred long miles away. They were dog–tired and, for the moment, recognizing that the mail was now one week to one month old, felt that a few more hours would not change the contents of the letters and packages to any remarkable degree

In fact, our gas mask hero had rested atop the pile of mail and had quickly fallen into a tired, sound sleep. The good colonel, bent on his mission and fortified with years of strict West Point discipline, strode into the barn. He didn't see the pile of mail. All he saw was his postal representative sleeping on the job, atop this precious pile of mail that the colonel wanted immediately disseminated to the front.

Carrying a swagger stick as an indelible part of his nature, he rushed over to the mountain of mail and angrily cracked our sleeping postman across the soles of his boots.

Our hero warily opened one eye and waited for the colonel to explode—and he did.

"What are you doing, sleeping with this mail in this condition?"

The postman, without opening his other eye, in a sort of offended but self–possessed voice, confessed, "Colonel, I wasn't sleeping. I was on a trip home."

The colonel began to sputter and began to ask for forgiveness. Backing away like Moses on Holy Ground before the Burning Bush, the colonel was saying, "I'm sorry," but thinking he was on the verge of winning his first mystical convert.

In the corners, behind the offending bags of mail, the rest of the mail workers were in hysterics. Life had won one of its biggest little victories; and these sorts of things seldom occurred in our military world.

***

Individual training required that the commanders anticipate how men would act under fire. This was also good for the individual. He needed to experience a condition similar to warfare in order to overcome some of the normal emotional shock attached to the sounds of life–killing live ammunition.

To make the knowledge realistic, a special "live–fire" training area was established. Several machine guns were set in sandbags at the end of an area about half the size of a football field. The guns were locked into a position where they could spray live ammunition at a regulated height. The field had to be crossed by a soldier crawling on his stomach under and through barbed wire, out of trenches and around pit holes. Land explosives were being fired that often covered the candidate with mud and water or plain dirt. All the time he was making his snakelike journey, the machine guns were firing live rounds at a discreet distance several feet above his backside.

Just about everyone in the Division made the trip through the "live–fire" course: doctors, chaplains; privates, sergeants, colonels and all the rest. To crawl out of a trench, to clamber over the edge and hear live bullets flying overheard and to see tractors speeding right over you in the air, to know that these lethal charges can destroy human flesh and life, required a bit of self–discipline, and I'm sure more than one man literally ruined his trousers during this operation.

Yet, I never heard of but one man standing up and getting hit. Evidently he had no self–control under these artificial kinds of conditions. One could reason that the officer in control was taking every kind of precaution. The guns were locked in and sandbagged in position. Firing would have stopped if some individual went berserk. But it did give one a taste of reality.

Another activity required that the individual walk into a U–shaped sort of fortification with walls three or four feet high. The individual was taught to pull the pin on a live grenade, lob it like a baseball at a distance in front of the fortification and then duck behind the wall. It was a simple procedure to execute, but occasionally a man became terrified at the very thought of having this much unleashed power in his vicinity and he would drop the live grenade. An alert NonCom had time to pick up the loose grenade and heave it outside the fortification. There are a few records of deaths due to such failures, but, in light of human emotional trauma, there were bound to be some.

Men do become irrational at times. Sometimes this irrationality is caused by plain boredom. I visited a man in a hospital in Italy who had been working with a buddy taking up land mines along the seacoast. It was a tedious job and they had removed hundreds of mines. His buddy, without warning, gave a slight curse, expressed his displeasure at this sort of boring repetition and literally threw a live mine over into a stack of other mines that had been retrieved from the sandy seashore. The live mine went off and in the explosion, the mine thrower was killed and his co–worker was badly injured.

Another time we had men unloading a truckload of mines in a little Italian town. One of the mines exploded and killed at least eight persons. The truck became a simple frame of steel and was blown straight up in the air in a narrow Italian street with six–story buildings on either side and landed four blocks from the scene of the explosion.

We picked up all the bits of flesh and bone we could find, and buried all of them in a common grave, but a few days later an American soldier eating his lunch, looked up at a tall school building and noted that the icicles on the house were red. He continued eating his lunch but suddenly realized icicles ought not to be red. He climbed to the top of the building and found a body almost intact. The dead man had been blown over one hundred fifty yards by the explosion that killed him. We never knew what caused the explosion, but, possibly a careless act on someone's part triggered devastation.

The interest span of soldiers who are being trained must also be considered. Training can be made practical and interesting—or it can be so boring men close their minds.

7
Unit Training

Joe Rhoan had begun to look like a soldier. He was tall, straight, lean, bronzed and walked with a thirty–inch step. His uniform was neat, well fitting and properly aged. He wore his hat at a military angle, just slightly on the rakish side, but not so far over it looked careless. His shoes shined with the practiced gleam that only soldiers recognize. He had learned to use every individual weapon well and was now ready to become a working member of a military team.

Sergeant Kovechni was no longer a drill sergeant. He had worked himself out of a job. Joe Rhoan had been assigned to his combat infantry platoon in the 349th Infantry Regiment, promoted to a Private First Class. When I next saw Joe, he was turning into the Company area along with his whole regiment. He had just finished a twenty–mile march. He was sweaty, tired, but not nearly as pooped as he was the day I met him at the troop train. When his unit was halted and given the command to "rest," he didn't even throw off his Infantry pack. He kept it on as we talked. He had gotten up at four o'clock that morning, eaten a hasty breakfast, and marched all day—and, to cap it off, they were going to march over to another area where field kitchens had been set up. There they would unload their packs, get an hour's rest and then march ten more miles that night.

"Only one man dropped out with bad feet. That's the best we have ever done," he reported.

In my own mind I was questioning the pressure of training, but I saw this same outfit later march fifty miles in a twenty–four hour period to surprise German columns that did not believe Infantry could do that sort of thing.

While Joe and I were talking, the chaplain of Joe's regiment came by. He was in battle gear, loaded up with a full field pack like everyone else; and in addition he was carrying a field kit that contained a cross, candlesticks, wine and an altar cloth to cover any makeshift altar he could find. This one was of his own design—and possibly became the forerunner of the more professional ones available to us later on.

After the chaplain had gone on his way, Joe told me the chaplain had marched with them all day and had moved about in the column to talk with and meet the men. "And, besides," Joe added, "When we took a rest break, he kept walking around talking with the men."

Joe told me he had mainly been occupied with squad and platoon training in the field. His squad and platoon was being taught how to launch an attack, how to keep together and communicate and how to operate in total darkness. They had crawled on their bellies for hours to surprise some of their unit who had temporarily become the "enemy." He learned to use cover of trees and terrain. He had been taught never to walk a ridgeline because he would be silhouetted against the sky and would become a perfect target for the enemy.

The skyline lesson was further dramatized about a year later. We had moved into North Africa and were doing division–type training in the mountains north of Sidi Bel Abbes, the home of the French Foreign Legion.

Our Commanding General was inspecting training and he saw some soldiers silhouetted against the skyline of one of the tall mountains. He ordered the soldiers to follow him. He led them about four miles down the steep sides of that mountain to Battalion Aid Station. He approached the two surprised Aid Men who were being trained to pick up wounded Infantrymen and take them to the Aid Station for treatment.

He ordered the medical men to lie down on the canvas stretchers. He then ordered the infantrymen who were guilty of exposing themselves against the skyline to pick up the men, take them the four miles back to the top of the mountain on stretchers and to bring them back again—and the general saw that his command was carried out.

As the old man said, "In actual combat, you infantrymen would have been casualties, and the Aid Men would have to carry you—if you had been wounded instead of killed."

Naturally, the story was told around the entire division area by nightfall and I never remember seeing one of our soldiers silhouetted against any skyline during our years of combat.

At about this same time, this same general did another rather flamboyant thing that became one of the best lessons soldiers can learn. Our bivouac areas in Africa lay at the foot of a huge range of mountains. There were no girls, only a few Arabs and a few more sheep.

Men were bored and during free time, would strike out for the top of the highest peak that overlooked our area. Some friends and I had climbed the mountain a half dozen times but we were not half as observant as our Commander. When he climbed up, he took in the sights and began to look around and to his horror, he found a pile of rocks where his soldiers (in typical

Kilroy fashion), had scratched their names—and horror of all horrors, a few had scratched the name of their unit.

Now, this was the worst breach of Army security. He had his Aide write down the name of every man whose name was inscribed on a rock. He got down to the foot of the mountain and ordered these men by name to report to his tent. He put the senior Name Scriber in charge, sent them up the mountain to get their rocks, bring the rock back down the mountain and then chisel off or hammer off every letter or number inscribed thereon. (After this lesson, I believe our division wrote less graffiti on privies than any other division since soldiers learned to write.)

Joe's unit was called back into formation and they marched off to chow. They were a rugged bunch. They were not tough or mean but comprised a good cross–section of the finest young men our nation could muster. They would be taught to fight in mock villages, given instructions in crossing rivers, landing on beaches, fighting in deserts and tropics, recognizing enemy aircraft, and communicating with their own aircraft.

Later, in the mountains along the central backbone of Italy, communication with friendly aircraft would save many lives. Rover Joes, as we called the team of four support aircraft, were available to us on call. They were loaded with rockets, machine guns and bombs. When we met strong enemy resistance, we would call the Rover Boys and they would come winging over and unload their arsenal at our direction.

Radio wasn't always as clear as we liked so we would dump a few rounds of phosphorus on the enemy target for identification purposes just as our planes showed up—but the Germans weren't so stupid. They learned to wait for the planes, too—and just as they showed up on the horizon they would dump a few rounds of phosphorus on one of our headquarters—which usually means one of the buildings left standing after the combat troops had worked the area over once or twice; sometimes twice, because occasionally we were pushed off our conquered ground by a German counter–attack and we had to take the same place again. In fact, there could be several exchanges in prolonged periods of siege and bad weather.

On the day in question, we had called the Rover Boys for help. They gallantly flew forward and the Germans dropped a round of phosphorus on one of our battalion headquarters. Rover Leader reacted in a typical manner. He waggled his wings and aimed straight for the phosphorus signal, not recognizing fellow Americans from four or five miles away. On the first run he unloaded his machine guns. Rover #2 and Rover #3 unloaded their rockets and Rover #4 added the *coup de grâce* with his bomb load. By this time, this Italian home was a maze of fallen timbers, dust from two–hundred–year–old mortar, and men were dying or dead.

One of the Battalion Chaplains knew that the Rover Boys would circle back again. #3 and #4 would unload their machine guns, and #1 would unload his rockets and #2 would unload his bombs. They would play this Merry–Go–Round for three cycles. The chaplain grabbed bed sheets from one of the bedroom drawers and rushed outside and made a big U.S. on the ground. Sure enough, #3 swung around and at a distance aimed straight at the smoking rubble and began firing.

The chaplain stood his ground, waving another sheet. Machine gun bullets zippered him in every direction. One would have thought he should have looked like Dick Tracy after the mob shot twenty holes in him, but only the end of one of his toes was shot off. When the plane got closer, it recognized the U.S., waved off the rest of the Rover Boys, got the right target in his sights and they unloaded the rest of their ordinance in the enemy. They flew back over the crippled headquarters, waggled their wings, radioed down a "We're sorry," and we began trying to retrieve the dead and wounded.

Joe Rhoan survived the night march and his company was soon spending weeks in the fields with the regiment. The squads had learned to work in platoons. Platoons had been welded into a company; companies had become a part of the Battalion. Now Battalions were learning to become a part of the Regimental fire assault team—and thus the Battle Division became a reality: Fifteen thousand Joe Rhoans doing their jobs, ranging from running a mimeograph machine to flying an observation plane.

8
Air Power

I have always been grateful that in combat, I knew the enemy had very little air power. I remember one bombing occasion most distinctly.

I knew nothing about combat, and nobody can tell you about the exact sounds and feel and nervous out–put in combat. I remember emotionally and exactly the first time I ever heard a bomb dropped in anger.

I was asleep in my tent and heard a shriek as if the fins on a bomb were clawing through the air. Without hesitation, without any pre–programming or pre–planning, I flipped off the cot, down onto the ground and glued myself to Mother Earth like a piece of adhesive.

I heard the first bomb explosion take place, and it landed at least four hundred yards from my tent. I heard the second shriek, and then the second explosion, and I immediately drew a line mentally between the first and the second; and the third bombing explosion corroborated the idea that I was right. The line headed right over my tent.

The tent flopped in the breeze.

I heard dirt and rock shredding the canvas and I heard the cutting sound of shrapnel coming through my tent.

The tent flopped in the breeze.

I heard the sixth explosion on past my tent, and for some reason, maybe because our troops usually strafed after a bombing run, I was so sure that the enemy place would return and strafe, that I jumped up out of the bedding roll and ran out the end of my tent. But in my emotional discomfiture, I had lost my orientation and I headed out the back of the tent, rather than the front. Now, the back of an officer's small wall, at least my small wall, was laced very tightly and stakes were driven down and the ropes were all tight and it was impossible to get out that end.

But not knowing in the darkness which way I was headed, I was determined to get out. Running as hard as I could with my best football motion, I drove my head into the tent wall and kept driving until finally the tent back was stretched like an arrow string with the arrow fully drawn.

When the tent would stretch no more, it sort of exploded. I was thrown backward, clear through the tent—out the front door. I had used some bomb fin guards as seats on my gravel front porch. As I was thrown back, I was knocking these fin guards right and left, and I could feel flesh being torn. I knew I was being hurt, but there was nothing I could do to stop myself. When I finally got myself under control, I dived for my ten–foot hole.

The men around there had kidded me about digging steps into the deep ditch. They thought that I, being a "man of faith," should not worry that much about my life. But, when I dived down into the double–duty ditch, I landed right on top of one of my neighbors who had decided that he could use a chaplain. Before I picked myself off of him, I looked up against the light of the sky and saw two more forms hurtling down on us.

I finally went back to sleep. When daylight broke, I went out to look at the huge crater that had been dug right beside my tent. It must have been thirty feet across and five or six feet deep. I retrieved a piece of shrapnel that had cut through my tent and landed in a tree on the opposite side. I still keep it as a souvenir, and a paperweight.

A man in our postal unit, sleeping two hundred yards away, was killed by shrapnel from the German bombs.

I could never understand how the enemy knew we were getting ready to attack, but they managed to get some sort of air power over us. I have been out when the enemy was dodging their planes over our lines, trying to bomb convoys or knock out bridges. I'd get in my foxhole and our own ack–ack would be firing at the planes; I've heard the falling shrapnel from our own ack–acks falling all around. I was never hit by any, but I have heard water sizzle when the hot shrapnel landed in it. So I am sure our own men have been hurt by our own shrapnel.

I think the most poignant thing I have ever seen in any enemy air attack was one winter night in the Apennines. We heard the ack–ack open up. I stepped out of my doorway and stood on a walk where I could look out across mountains covered with deep snow, lying majestic and glistening and still on this quiet, clear, freezing winter night. The moon was shining brightly, we could see the outline of the enemy plane as the shrapnel burst around it and as the pin–points of light from the searchlights picked it up like a moth transfixed by a moving blade of light. It was silhouetted against the dark sky like a toy in a show window display back home.

I don't think I have ever felt so closely identified with anyone in my life. As I watched this pilot twisting his plane and turning it, winging it over and over, climbing for the sky, trying to evade the searchlights, trying to survive, trying to live, trying to get back to his own territory, I began to sweat.

For a moment, I felt that I was in the plane; and I shared his same apprehension, and fear, and anxiety, as I watched him clawing around in the air. I could imagine his fear when the lights lighted up the plane like noonday and it looked like some toy out there in the sky. The ack–ack was always just a little behind him. It always seemed to me that if it had moved up just a little further, it would have blown him out of the sky. But I watched him for what seemed like hours, and yet I know it was only a matter of minutes, as he fled toward the north, throwing his plane from side to side, in the valleys and over the tops of the mountains, going straight up and coming straight down, twisting over and over like an insect burning in a flame.

I have often wondered if he survived, if he is alive today in Germany, telling about the night that he ran his "Washboard Charlie" milk run up through the Apennines and finally climbed out of the deep mountain passes and crossed over to Bologna.

I watched our own planes many times. They were like men who were driving trucks. They hauled bombs to the enemy. Early in the morning they would start out, hundreds of bombers; and you watched them come home in the evening, with a few less bombers than they had when they started. I watched our planes bomb Cassino; I saw them come over in deliberate groups, dropping tons and tons and tons of bombs.

But really in the effort to destroy Cassino, we made it a more formidable fortress.

I am always impressed with the ability of man to survive. I stood in the forest, outside of Florence. We had laid fifteen hundred guns, aimed at this mountainside and for thirty minutes we fired high–explosive ammunition into the mountains and forest, hoping to kill Germans who were in their fortifications; laying waste these beautiful trees, so our men could get through, and get up and get over them. And I am not sure whether we helped our men or not in this process.

I traveled this road many times after this and I never ceased to be amazed to see how we would level whole forests, and cut the trees down like some giant had bulldozed them over. The enemy could survive and sit in their bunkers on top of the mountains with their field of fire spread out over the valleys below and cover a space like a fan, and yet somehow or other our infantrymen could go through this blazing hell, and get close enough to a bunker to throw in a hand grenade, or set a heavier explosive and blow them to kingdom come.

9

At Sea

We had finished our troop training at Camp Gruber, Oklahoma. We had been tested in maneuvers in Louisiana, and all of us realized we were nearing pay dirt when our troop trains pulled into Newport News, Virginia. The train followed tracks right into a brand–new staging area.

There were large numbers of barracks around and we already had an advance group of people who had decided where each unit should go and there were road guides to show us. We unpacked, looked over our buildings, and began our regular and continuing duties, with an air of expectancy as we waited for orders to go overseas. We didn't know if it would be one day or two days, or ten. But we were ready and found that we must get our equipment in shape, we must take care of any last–minute personal matters, sign wills, get ready for combat. Waiting is difficult, but we were soon ready.

Every war is very secret. We drove down to the harbor and saw hundreds of Liberty ships riding at anchor and we knew they could not stay there long.

In typical Army Chaplain fashion, we found the mess hall first, chapels second, and then looked for places of recreation for the men. There were several theaters and a large new gymnasium. The second night we arranged fights and with a little wheedling and encouragement, we were able to fix up a pretty good fight card, and I was given the job of refereeing the matches and getting them moving out on time. We got the band and it was a wonderful evening. We used huge boxing gloves and nobody was badly hurt.

But then the word came that we were leaving the next afternoon. My staff was called in and, at that time, I was the assistant division chaplain. We were told that an advance group would fly over, and the rest of us would come by ship. And, after they didn't want a chaplain going over with the advance party, and since the senior chaplain of our division was going with the division headquarters, I asked if I might go with one of the infantry troop ships because there were only two chaplains available for one regiment and that left a whole battalion and one troop ship without a chaplain. So I planned to go overseas with one of the battalions of the 351st Infantry.

I was given the number of my ship, the time of departure of my troop train, and I was to get all my equipment together. At that time, I was already a major, which was a very high ranking for an infantry battalion.

But I showed up at the troop train, with helmet, dressed as near like a combat soldier as I could. I had a huge barracks bag filled with clothing, bedding roll and miscellaneous. The whole pack of gear must have weighed a hundred and twenty–five pounds. I also had a small musette bag, filled to the brim and strapped tight. I had a huge raincoat, with a liner, plus a field jacket, and a chaplain's kit.

We had ridden about fifteen or twenty miles into the city on the rambling troop train and unloaded right at one of the large wharves. As we got off, one of the men ran down to me and said he had heard I was a chaplain and they wanted to take my picture as I boarded the troop ship. I had a cross on my helmet, so I bravely started up the gangplank with approximately two hundred pounds of equipment, struggling even with my six foot, two hundred pound size, up the narrow gangplank. It took all my energy to get to the ship and nobody gave me any help. Just as I got to the top, and the photographer was getting ready to snap my picture, I gave one grunt with all this equipment and the flash went off; my helmet fell down over my eyes, and I know I became the proverbial "Sad Sack" that later was publicized in the comics.

Needless to say, I never saw a copy of that picture in the newspaper of any signal files. I have a feeling I looked everything but a soldier, but I went on down into the bowels of the ship to a room with two infantry officers.

I had a good bunk and the surroundings were very comfortable if you liked living inside a tin can for several weeks. I lay and waited until everybody was aboard and finally we began to pull out into the harbor. We were told we would wait there until time for the convoy to leave.

I took sort of an inspection tour around the ship. I found out there were about a thousand men aboard and there were only about five hundred and fifty bunks. Half of the men would sleep at night and the other half in the daytime; hot bunking was the term given to such arrangements. So I went around looking at the barracks, looking at the bunks, went up on deck and found five hundred men standing around on the deck, trying to get in some windward position where they could keep from freezing. The other half went down and occupied themselves inside the bowels of the ship.

All of us listened as the convoy started, and we heard the ship's motor start pumping and throbbing and we knew we were out to sea. We sort of felt we were on a great adventure. We were not then able to recognize the dangers or difficulties, and we settled down to a good night's sleep, before we were to find out what life aboard the ship was like. We found out at breakfast time—there were two huge steam kettles in the troop compartment. Breakfast wasn't so bad because you would either have two big pots of cereal or you could scratch one cereal and have one big pot of hot chocolate, and we had the best hot chocolate aboard the ship that I have ever known. Then came lunch and dinner, dinner was the main meal on board ship; lunch was more of less cold cuts and crackers and bread and sandwiches and that sort of thing; but at night, it was stew.

The first ten days out stew was not so bad, but after you have had stew, and stew, and stew, and stew—it began to get a little monotonous. We reasoned that some broad–beamed executive sitting in some swanky office chair said, as he looked at the plans for the Liberty ship, "Well, those Liberty ships don't need to take a lot of cooking equipment, they'll only be aboard three weeks or four weeks, maybe only two weeks."

I think if we could have had that broad–beamed individual aboard after two weeks of slumgullion, we'd have probably put him in one of those steam vats and cooked *him*.

In fact, after we were out to sea for about seven days, there was so much unhappiness over the food, I had two other officers appointed to check with the ship's captain about the food situation. Our first approach was to ask for an inventory of all the food that had been put aboard ship or the transport.

We found out that the merchant seamen ate about three different kinds of meat every meal, had a choice of two of three desserts. We concluded they were living like kings while we were down in the bowels of the ship, living on stew. We found out that there had been plenty of beef put aboard. The commander began to see our point of view that either we got the meat that had been put aboard, including steaks, regardless of how they were cooked, and that we got a variety of vegetables, or when the ship docked in Casablanca, there was going to be trouble at the wharf; and the captain would be right in the middle of it. We were determined to report to our representatives there.

Well, we finally brought the captain around. Steaks were served often and fresh vegetables and desserts. The men had appreciated the position I had taken in their behalf and they attended services with regularity far beyond their religiosity.

We began to plan our own entertainment, and we canvassed the ship for talent. It was not surprising that we found much varied abilities aboard this one ship. When the evenings were good, we would get up on deck and have a program, or we would have prizefights, or theater, or singing of music down in the hold.

We were always a little nervous on the deck, and many of us would go up and keep a sharp lookout for German submarines. There was always someone rumoring that several ships could not keep up with the convoy, but the convoy was going so slow I don't know how they could have kept from staying up.

There were rumors that some of the ships had been picked off by German submarines. We did see flares going up at night and we heard ash cans exploding or shelling. We could look at the ash cans on our own ship and realize that there could be trouble.

The old sailor's story was circulated that in about five days we would reach the mail buoy and pick up the mail. There were a couple of comedians aboard ship who wrote newsletters every day in the form of wireless telegrams—there were such things as, "Fala, Roosevelt's dog, had taken over the country and that anybody who didn't move very fast would have trouble; especially if he had a wooden leg."

There was one rumor that the Pope's son had asked for a divorce from some prominent movie star.

We found our biggest problem was when rough seas made half our passengers seasick. Some people get seasick for a day or two out, 'til they get out away from the shore and then they become accustomed to the sea; they settle down and they eat and they live fairly well. But we had some men who were sick all the time they were on the ship and the saddest part was that down in the hold these five hundred men slept in one huge room, which was locked up and closed off at night. Sometimes the air conditioner worked and sometimes it didn't and men were vomiting all over the place. To be locked up in that hold with the putrid air and five hundred sweating men in a hot steel bin was something that even the toughest stomach had trouble accepting.

It was a rough way to get to combat. But sure enough, we did get to Casablanca in good shape. There was not a great deal of hatred for merchant marines or the seamen or the captain of the ship; things were going well and we had worked out a good routine.

We all concluded we had had a good trip over because we made it.

10

Kill 'Em Dead

Combat is seldom like the movies.

One of the most unusual commanders we had was a colonel in one of our regiments. He was typical West Pointer and certainly of the old school. He had persistence, even a stubbornness and a will to win that came directly out of his West Point training of duty, honor, country. Duty was his great religion; he believed that a man must do his duty above everything else. He trained his men and his officers with ruthlessness and a dedication that belonged to a man who clearly knew his purpose. He directed his men without one whit of wavering. Whenever there was a rough task in combat, he was one man who was called on to lead.

I graduated from the Army War College, Command General Staff School, was Chaplain at the Infantry Center for three years, and one of my tasks was to learn something about the line officer's concept of strategy and of tactics. I heard a great deal about flanking movements, about the element of surprise; but when we hit the enemy I usually saw a direct frontal attack on his position. I doubt that less than half a dozen times the enemy was surprised when we made an attack. Usually, he seemed to know we were coming, and was ready for us.

So what we usually did was hit the enemy on the nose like a prize fighter battering an opponent until his defensive nose was completely ruined. When we had killed all his combat soldiers, or when the enemy soldiers had surrendered, we were then able to walk into and through his defensive positions.

On one of our last attacks in Italy, the enemy soldiers had sagely ensconced themselves inside a mountain; they had tunneled through the peak in honeycomb fashion. They had built tremendous fortifications in the front of it. They had our field completely covered with machine guns, mortar, and heavy artillery fire. We were closely watched day by day as we prepared to attack their position. Finally the time came for the jump–off; and by coincidence, we found that a young lieutenant colonel had reported for duty.

As was often the case, the battalion that was going to launch the major attack needed a combat commander. As an aside, I have found that one of the most expendable leaders in combat was the lieutenant colonel that led the battalion. More often, this young commander had to get it where it was supposed to go. This is not the theory taught in school. He is supposed to stand back and send his soldiers in, but because of the tremendous stress of combat it's difficult to get men to fight. And so the battalion commander often led the spearhead companies into combat and often he caught one of the first rounds of ammunition that was fired, and so many of these young brave battalion commanders were killed. I buried them in the many cemeteries we opened behind the combat lines, so we were always short of battalion commanders.

But to get back to my young lieutenant colonel who had been chosen to lead the attack. He was sort of a dual personality. He had gone to a religious school to be trained as a clergyman, but while he was there he took ROTC training. He found himself commissioned a second lieutenant when he got out of school, and a reserve second lieutenant's pay was very helpful for a preacher so he continued as a line officer. When World Was II came along, this fellow by nature, by teaching ability, by plain tenacity and will, was able to become a very fine instructor in the infantry training command. And before long, in the wartime push, he had gotten to the rank of lieutenant colonel. There were times when he thought he ought to transfer to the chaplain's service, but because he was probably doing better as a line officer than he would have as a chaplain, he continued in the training command.

As expected, when a man gets rank, he is assigned to do the work that goes with it. Because of the tremendous loss of combat officers in Italy, he found himself under orders to report to the combat theater. I am sure he didn't think much about this, thinking he was very well qualified by training to take up the job. As most officers before they have really had their nose bloodied in combat, he probably knew very little about war. He took the assignment and reported to our division, where he was immediately assigned to Colonel West Point's battalion. Before he had unpacked his battle gear, he was briefed and was told the exact hour and minute he was to take his battalion up the mountain against the enemy. This was one of those hammers against anvil affairs and he was the ball peen of the hammer.

The new commander–clergyman jumped off at the scheduled hour with his battalion and immediately all his attacking companies ran into a minefield. Mines began to explode, men were blown to pieces, and the enemy knew that someone was out there. With guns that had already been zeroed in, they began to methodically pulverize the entire valley and the approaches to the mountains.

Before our new commander knew what hit him, out of some seven hundred men, within a short space of an hour and a half, he had lost more than half his troops. He felt that his losses were such that he had to return to friendly territory. He came back, and ran head–on into the regimental commander's rugged will and determination.

The colonel, in best military tradition thundered, "Reorganize your battalion and attack again."

Well, this young lieutenant colonel—half clergyman—half line officer, could not see the moral value or the utility of an attack with a battalion already decimated. He asked the colonel to defer, but the colonel wasn't about to defer. He had a job to do and he again ordered the man to attack.

When he wouldn't, he was immediately placed under house arrest up in the combat area. The lieutenant colonel's Executive Officer was ordered to take the battalion in. Well, it so happens the battalion did make it across the field because I guess the first attack had already exploded all the mines. They got up and took the mountain and by daylight they were in control of the entire mountain.

I remember spending some hours talking with this lieutenant colonel who felt very sad that he had been put in such a bind but I had little sympathy for his predicament. If you are a combat officer you fight, if you are a non–combatant, then you are a non–combatant, but you don't get the two mixed up. When you receive the pay, the rank and the allowances of a combat officer, you live up to the requirements and the exigencies that face a combatant.

Finally, out of deference to the fact that this man was literally a clergyman and because of the brutality and shock of the first combat assignment given to him, he was given a chance to resign his commission and return to the United States. I don't think he even had a scratch, but I did receive a piece from the local state paper telling about this clergyman, "who had just returned from combat in the ferocious Italian Campaign," and, how because he was a clergyman, he had gotten out of the service, but that he had led a battalion on the attack on the Gothic line and all this sort of thing.

Well, my first reaction was to write to the citizens in his hometown and tell them what really happened. I realized most of us live on a certain amount of "fluff." We present our best side to everybody and most of us would not like the actual truth really known about us and our capabilities.

***

I never ceased to be amazed at the courage of men in combat. I remember a colonel who later became general, who seemed to be completely without nerves in the midst of an impossible living Hell. Our support tanks were called up to fire into enemy bunkers to protect the infantrymen who were going across an open area, but the tankers felt that they would be so vulnerable, they wouldn't do it. The tank commander decided it was impractical for their tanks to go into this area.

The infantry colonel said, "If I could take my jeep in there, would you follow me?" With the Tank Commander's affirmative answer the colonel gets up and sits on the front of the jeep, with his feet on the bumper, armed with nothing but a swagger stick and a pistol at his side; with his driver driving him, he rode right into the combat area, straight into the enemy fire. Of course the tanks could do nothing but follow him. I think many of us would say that this is completely impractical, but the colonel did it and the position was won.

The Aid Station was using an Old Italian farmhouse and had very little of what one would expect a hospital to look like. A few stretchers lay on the ground, and a dozen extra stretchers were stacked up around the door. Three wounded men occupied the stretchers inside the building. Two of them would go back with the ambulance that came in. The other would remain until another ambulance came.

The doctor was a timid-looking major, but was one of the most respected men I have ever seen in combat. The line officers, troops, and the chaplain talked with him in a tone that bespoke admiration. They listened to what he had to say. They shared with him their fears and their hopes.

I told the surgeon I had not really seen much close–up combat and I wanted to learn a little more about it. I didn't give him any idea of why I had come up to the Aid Station, but the real burden of his advice was that these men were pushed beyond any concept of human endurance. Those who managed to survive were continually left in battle until they either died or got what was called a "million dollar" wound.

This confirmed my own feeling, because I remember talking to a soldier one evening who had been brought in to the division clearing company and his first question was about the nature of his wounds. He didn't want to know if he was going to lose a leg. He wasn't asking if he would have to face surgery, or if he would be maimed the rest of his life. What he really wanted to know without asking the question was, "Do I have a 'million dollar' wound; will I be sent back to the United States and be able to go home and not return to combat?" Would they send him home? It was a great disappointment to most men to be wounded in combat and then recover and be sent back to combat. Human nature fights danger and when you are continually pushed back into a dangerous area, the men begin to feel that it is unfair and unjust.

Just about the time we had finished a C-ration supper, and finished our coffee, we heard a few shouts outside. An infantry company had been relieved at the front–line and was placed in reserve. Before long the company was filtering into the aid station to get hot coffee, to warm up their own C-rations. In the freezing and cold ground, they dug themselves shallow foxholes. They were the typical combat soldiers who returned from the front; their faces were thin and gaunt, most of them had sort of scraggly beards, and their eyes had a hollow look that you see in men who have really suffered front-line action.

I watched and listened till I was so sleepy I couldn't keep my eyes open. I pulled up my bedding roll and was soon asleep. It must have been about two hours later when I heard voices. The battalion surgeon and the company commander had broken open a bottle of medicinal alcohol. They talked until daylight and I lay listening in my bedding roll.

The battalion surgeon was sort of the "father confessor and compassionate friend." He listened to the company commander as he poured out his frustrations and hurt. He was an older type—having survived many days in combat. I never was able to determine if combat or if years had so aged him.

I learned the greatest lesson from him that I have ever learned of combat soldiers. As I lay there in my bedding roll and listened to them talk, I heard him tell about their last attack. Made a little more talkative and less intimidated by a few drinks of alcohol, in his tired and worn condition from days of face–to–face combat with an enemy under tremendously difficult conditions, he recalled rather languidly and pitifully the story.

"We left at three o'clock in the morning," the Company Commander recalled. "In the old days, we would have left just one hour before daylight, but with all these new men, with the situation like it is, I thought we better start plenty early. I lined them all up single file and I told them that the real success of this mission lay in getting to the attack point at the proper time. Now, I wanted them to stay behind each other, stay in single file, and if they did lose sight of the man in front of them of if they could not touch him, they should stop and quietly call out 'lost contact'. I knew they were nervous and I gave the command to move out. We hadn't gone fifty yards, till I heard 'lost contact'. I called the column to a halt. I went back and hit each man on the rump, moved the next man up close to him, and after about twenty minutes I had the company organized again and started out. We had not gone another fifty yards till I heard 'lost contact'. The result was that it was almost daylight before we got to the place where we were to attack. In the old days, with my well–trained company, I would have gotten there in less than one hour, and I would have been ready to jump off and take on the enemy. Instead, I sent back three of my best sergeants to pick up the stragglers, knowing full well they would have to use whatever force was necessary to bring them up. In the meantime, we attacked the enemy and with this handful of men, we crossed their fortifications and their caves and we were on top of the mountain. That's when all Hell broke loose. They sent us back down here, and a fresh company came to take our place."

A few days before, I had stopped at a house several miles from the front. I had seen some soldiers there, and thought, in my job as chaplain, I should stop by and see them. But I had barely gotten out of my jeep when I saw another jeep approaching at a fast pace. Two sergeants got out; they had their carbines at ready position and I heard them release their safety latches—one stood on one side of the house, the other went to the back—and yelled inside to the men to come out.

Soldiers gradually drifted out. One sergeant stood there with his rifle trained on them and the other went into the house and brought out two more stragglers who had thought they might be able to remain behind. They put them out on the road in front of them. The two sergeants got into their jeep and told the stragglers to march toward the front lines.

I never doubted that the sergeants would have shot any man who gave them any trouble. It never occurred to me as I watched this drama that they were doing anything but what had been done in combat. I understood something of why the stragglers had lost courage, but I also understood that in battle there is little human end except to win. When combat had gone this far, every human life is on the line.

Combat is a continual revelation of human limitation. During the worst parts of combat we were courts–martialing fifty to seventy–five men per month for desertion in the face of the enemy and these men were getting fifty to seventy–five years in prison for their failure.

My commanding general called me and several of his staff people into his office and asked what we could do to help men accept the importance of their combat jobs. I have always been strong for proper orientation and team spirit. When men in a squad know each other, they will do better out of a sense of pride, if for no other reason.

We discussed and discussed, but it became clear men deserted because they were afraid of getting killed and it was calmer in the rear areas. Usually, an Italian family would welcome the GI and if there was a daughter all the better.

So, all of us—along with the commander, came to the conclusion that for the first offense we would sentence any AWOL or deserting GI (if we caught him before he got out of Division Territory) to a prison compound within range of enemy shell fire. Every sentenced GI could dig a hole as deep as he chose, sand bag it, make it as comfortable as possible under that situation—and we gave him his own C-rations which he had to prepare—and before long we had men going back to the front lines for they began to feel more protected there than in our prison.

The next morning I arose early and walked out of the Battalion Aid Station, and in a sheltered place behind a mountain lay all the men who survived the Infantry company attack. Two men lay in each shallow, covered with a GI blanket. There had been a light snow during the night. These men lay there covered only with their one wool blanket and their light blanket of snow. Little bits of steam came from their nostrils as they breathed, and bits of ice had collected on the edge of their blanket around their nose and mouth.

Before long these guys began to rouse from sleep and they were heating water to shave off week–old beards. Stripped to their olive–colored undershirts, they exchanged pleasantries, reinforced their combat stories and suggestions with mild obscenities that men come to use when only men are present, and they were ready for breakfast when someone yelled that hot coffee and cereal was ready. They were glad to be alive.

Not one man had a cough or cold, and I smiled for I was sure many of their wives or mothers were filled with fear when they were caught in a cold drizzle back home.

11

OUR TRIP OVER

I have seen men dumped into the maelstrom of war like iron ore dropped into a flaming furnace, but for most soldiers, combat creeps inexorably upon the combatant. He knows it is coming, but it's hard to tell how far away it is.

I spent an evening aboard our transport on our way to Italy, talking with Joe Rhoan. We were both uneasy about the trip. There was grim foreboding as we walked up the gangplank, we both agreed, but the mental and psychological preparation for combat is long and difficult.

Joe told me about saying good–by to his aunt. She had been like a mother to him for more than ten years, and in a real sense, she knew he was all she had left. She hadn't liked his short hair, his polished boots, his new and finicky way with his room, but she almost flipped when she heard the language he had picked up in his training days—a language that had become so natural to him that he used in front of his aunt without excuse.

Then he began to recount the evening he told her good–by. His voice trembled and tears came in his eyes as he recalled how she held fiercely to him. Her fingers clawed into his skin and she began to weep, and over and over, she said, "I will never see you again! I'll never see you again! I'll never see you again."

He kissed her hair, pulled away and grabbed the streetcar for the train station. When he finally reached the station and waited for his train to our Port of Debarkation, he sat in the shadows and wept unashamedly but quietly. He admitted he didn't understand why he wept, but there was something final and grim about this stage in life.

Joe and I sat quietly at the bow of the ship and talked. The waves slurped at the side of the ship as the old tub moved slowly through the Atlantic. We could look across and count at least twenty other ships in our convoy as their dark hulks loomed up from the sea—and we thought about German submarines lying dead, seeing the same things we could see.

And I began to tell Joe about my farewell.

I remember the day they told us we were going overseas. The general called all the officers together and gave us the word. We didn't know where, but we would soon be on our way.

I went up the drive toward the house and Eugenia knew what it was. I didn't even have to tell her. I just said "I don't know where nor when,—but I guess it will be pretty soon."

We both looked out across the lawn of our lovely, comfortable Spanish–type home to the officers club and the swimming pool. Then we sort of took in the beautiful room in which we were sitting. It was the best home we had had since we married over three years before. We had been caught up in the growing army and a rat placed in a specially–built maze couldn't have lived any more erratically than we did, as we tried to cram a life into the few years the army spared us to be together. We both looked at the nicely polished floors, and thought how much we would have loved to stay there for a long, long time.

She knew I wanted to go and she wouldn't even try to hold me as long as it had come naturally. If I had volunteered for combat duty she would have been heartbroken, but this was what we had been madly training for—this was it.

We both recalled the fourth of December 1941, when I was alerted for the Philippines. We had gone through all the emotions we would have to go through at a parting before the Japs made a trip to the Islands impossible with the bombing of Pearl Harbor.

I was pretty dumb in those days. I felt like I had been cheated of a noble adventure and rather wished they had held off till I got there. After two years of war, I marveled at my naïveté, but then I was only a child in the way of battle.

Now we tried to think how long I would be gone. I said one year as glibly as I would have said one week of maneuvers. She said two years and stuck to her story. I felt I knew more about current events than she, but it turned out she was much wiser; though only half as wise as she could have been.

Getting ready to climb the gangplank was one day of hurry–up followed by another that called for faster action. The pace was terrific and the rumors flew thick and fast. The best one said it was all a dry run and was far from the real thing. But the day came to say good–by to Eugenia.

I had planned to take her in my arms, tell her I loved her and would be back soon. It worked all right up to the last day. We ate lunch at the club and hurriedly finished packing. I packed the car for her to go home to her parents. We locked the house and forgot part of my field equipment. It took another hour to get the key. We drove out to Breckenridge Park and sat and talked and our sadness began to thicken like a heavy cloud. Finally, it came time to drive to the train.

I put on my field equipment, my steel helmet and we looked toward the hundreds of troops marching toward the train parked at the Fort Sam siding. I kissed her good–by but she wouldn't go. I told her she had to go. She started the car and backed out into the street, started sobbing then drove off. I saw her body shaken by the sobs and watched the car till she drove away.

I turned toward the train, my eyes brimming, my throat full, my stomach in turmoil and my heart actually hurting. One of the chaplains came down to see me off but I only nodded to him and went off. If I had had Hitler in my power at that moment, I would have punched each eye out separately. I would have used pliers to pull out his nails. I would have beaten his head against a telephone post till he would have been one soft bloody mass in my eager hands.

At that moment, he was the totality of all the evil, the heartache, the living terror rampant in the world. He represented something so inanimate I couldn't hate him, but something that was so definite, I could have cruelly destroyed him in a manner such as I had never thought possible before.

Joe looked at me like I was sort of insane, but he had an inkling of my feeling. We watched the ocean for almost an hour without saying more than a hundred words, but bound together in a sort of friendship that needed no conversation. We stayed there until men began to move out on deck from their "hot bunks" below and it was time for Joe to sleep his turn. He saluted and went below.

I returned his salute and talked with the new shift of soldiers who had been sleeping for eight hours and were now trying to get fresh air back into their lungs after living through the staleness of decks below.

Joe and I got together for cup of coffee just before we debarked in Casablanca. We watched the harbor come into view, marveled at the hulls of sunken ships, and were enthralled by the myriad of different people who stood and worked on the docks as we approached.

He admitted that his heart beat faster, for soon we would have a whole new continent under our feet. We knew combat had passed this part of the world. Rommel's Army was imprisoned. Allies were in charge, but we knew there were still Stuka attacks—and, most of all, the Arabs looked to us like they might not all be our friends. We had seen too many movies of the Casbah.

I did see Joe one day as I tramped through the streets of Casablanca, but he was so busy checking equipment and getting ready for our trip on the French "40 & 8," (forty men on eight horses) that he hadn't had much time to become more apprehensive. When we did get aboard these little cars and headed for Oran, I looked him up and he admitted he was now worrying about the situation that lay ahead.

Oran was one for the books. Balloons were anchored all over the place by a one–thousand–foot slender cable, and twice when we were there, the Germans tried to bomb the harbor. One night they got one ship, but all they did was make us more aware that we were now playing for keeps.

I visited Joe's unit and his chaplain and I looked him up. This time he wasn't apprehensive about the war. He had a commander who spent most of his time hitting the bottle and the rest of the time, at all hours of the day or night, he had officers, enlisted men and Red Cross girls on the carpet for some imagined infraction. He was giving the troops hell and Joe slyly, in a confidential aside to me, inferred that the enemy couldn't be worse. The staff said nothing, but I verified the situation and when I went back to Division Headquarters that evening I went to see the general and told him what I thought I had found. He sent his own people up to verify and Joe's unit had a new commander in two days.

Then came the day we boarded British transports— and they didn't tell us where we were going. However, only a guy who didn't read the papers would not know he had to be headed for Anzio, Naples, Malta, or maybe Sicily, but the Lord was kind to us—and on this trip we didn't have much time to be apprehensive.

We had the roughest weather I have ever seen in the Mediterranean. Fourteen-foot waves slammed our ship like it was a cork. We dined in the British Navy dining room with white, freshly-ironed tablecloths, sterling service, and uniformed waiters—the waves were so violent dining was an impossibility.

What could have been a wonderful experience was ruined by the weather plus one thing. I went down into the lower decks to see how our men were fairing; down there they had one steam pot in a tropical setting. The cooks were stirring the pot and the sweat dropped off their arms into the pot. I decided then and there that England still had an upper class and lower class society. We survived and finally were told we were headed to Naples.

Naples was one for the books, too. Its harbor was not only filled with sunken hulls, but we had bombed most of the dock area to smelly rubble. What we hadn't ruined, the Kraut Air Force had finished. When they transported us from the ships to our first bivouac, we were introduced to the complete destructiveness of modern war. Children sat on dirty quilts inside caves, under bridges, in rubble, and makeshift homes built right into the rubble. They all seemed hungry, and that night we filled tin pails carried by hungry Italian children with the remains from our coffee cups and our plates—the coffee into one gallon buckets with a wire handle and the scraps of food into another tin bucket. (At the time, these seemed like the only reasonable things to do, but I keep waiting for some new Mussolini to lead the Italians to hate the Americans by recalling the day when they "ate American scraps and the Capitalistic Americans ate an abundance of beefsteak and sweets.")

We didn't stay in Naples long. We got new trucks and headed into the hinterland. Now, we could hear the big guns booming. We could hear an occasional bomb and see ack-ack light the sky. We trained some more, and then sent our first troops to Cassino and had our first battle casualties.

Joe came by my office. His unit had already been on the front for five days and he wanted me to know he was a veteran. He recounted the difficulty of getting into battle positions in the dead of the night.

He reported, "Everybody was tense and the first night our guards filled two lister bags with holes." (These were water bags made of duck, holding about thirty gallons of water. They were suspended on a tripod and had faucets for men to use to get a drink.) "At night, one of these lister bags loomed up in the darkness and a trigger–happy guard challenged it and when it didn't give the password it was fired into. One guy missed the bag completely when he fired, but two other guards did a good job and then were terrified as the water gurgled out. We never quite got used to jumpy guards killing a cow who happened to wander into camp, or collecting a few more 'lister bags scalps', but it was a matter of serious concern when one of our own men was killed by a guard who didn't take long enough to find out, 'Friend or Foe'."

I distinctly remember the first time I went anywhere close to the front lines. I went up to the cemetery at Cassino to bury one of our soldiers. No one had told me about French Ghoums in their red uniforms. No one had reported, "We had Red-Fezzed troops fighting with the French and with us."

Couple all that with my feeling that I may be reading the map wrong in this entirely new territory, my uneasiness that the guns firing might be incoming rather than outgoing, and my own feeling of nakedness as I drove. (I must have had a heart beat rate twice normal). I stopped several times along the way and talked to troops and finally made it to the cemetery. I was shocked by the lack of emotion I observed in the cemetery chaplain. My heart was beating twice as fast while his beat twice as slow as we stood talking, surrounded by hundreds of graves.

I found later that when you are in combat long enough, normalcy is a relative term.

Then we moved into battle position. A burned-out German plane lay like a decomposed bird on the hill near our camp. We used smoke to conceal our bridge across the Garigliano River. At Gaeta, every time I went across that bridge I felt like death was breathing down my neck.

I think the Germans didn't have much ammunition, for they fired spasmodically at crossing traffic and at the bridge. They also may have feared our own artillery retaliation. Our infantry troops were ranged along the perimeter of the mountain, while the Germans sat in the high peaks observing almost every move we made.

We ran our patrols out at night and pushed our forward lines out as far as possible. We soon zeroed in on the German observation post and now, for target practice, we tried to hit the forward foxholes of the

German troops or tried to lob our artillery shells into their observation posts.

I found that I was safe riding a motorcycle along the roads at the foot of the German-held mountains. The MPs had liberated an English motor bike and they made it available to me as I visited up there. I paid my usual visit to Joe Rhoan.

He was comfortably located inside an old quarry. He had made three patrols and was beginning to think of himself as a veteran combat soldier—and he let me know he was now classifying men like me as Rear Echelon Commandos, but he did tell me one of the typical stories of our day.

It seems that, "A farmer came to his company commander several nights before and wanted to be paid for some harness he had furnished the U.S. Army. The Company Commander was in the dark about why we needed harness but the Italian informed him that our pack mules needed harness and—he had sold a beautiful set of harnesses to an American soldier. The soldier had given him a professional looking IOU and he showed it to the Army Captain—and there it was—an IOU signed by Tom Mix."

I later found we paid the farmer for his harness and Joe, who knew the smart-aleck American, swore the harness was shipped back to an Iowa farm in a properly wrapped package for the U.S. Mail.

Joe also gave me a soldier's eye view of our Assistant Brigadier General. He was the man who had already distinguished himself at the Rapido and who was soon to become the Division Commander and a major general.

He was a huge, burly man and he loved infantry soldiers. He went around talking to them and he had a way of slapping them on their back that literally staggered them. Joe's comment, "How does he get away with that crap," was not withdrawn even after my answer reminded him of his aunt in Pittsburgh.

It was in such a situation as this that one of the most unusual Easter services took place that was ever chronicled in the annals of war—Oscar was a fine Lutheran Chaplain. He spoke German like a native. On Easter morning in 1944, he set up his PA-system speakers facing the Germans and his American troops. He conducted his service in both German and English. His choir needed no translations. For a few minutes the guns on the Garigliano River and the German-held heights were silent.

We all watched Cassino bombed to rubble. We were bombed ourselves. Our wounded began to fill our hospitals and I began to bury the dead in increasing numbers. But then came the time we were finished sitting and we started out to climb the mountain in front of us.

I had gone to the Division Headquarters briefing and I knew the time for the TOT (time on target). (In this exercise we aimed every gun in the Division at a particular point on the mountainside and at an exactly synchronized time, we fired all of these guns at once and kept firing them till we had finished the specified time and specified rounds.) Then the infantry moved forward.

Theoretically, the enemy was dead or shocked, but it was always surprising how fast they could recover and how much fire they could deliver on our advancing infantry. Surviving German guns opened up. German mortars began to sputter, German hand grenades began to explode along with our own American grenades. Rifles from both sides cracked, machine guns tore at the darkness, and the German paper cutters or Zip Guns were soon distinguishable from our own machine guns.

Battle Rattle

I stand in awe and wonder as I have seen what the American soldier has done for he always seemed to be on the offensive—and was always in a very vulnerable position. We always let the other guys start the war and we begin our fight at a serious disadvantage—but, because of the quality of the American soldier, and material, "We go on and win."

12
Aberrations

The colonel was a big, strong, and attractive man. He had graduated from West Point in the Thirties and had soon resigned his commission and began living the life of a country gentleman in the South. (I always had the feeling he left the service to please his wife.)

World War II came along and he came back on Active Duty. He was a very competent lieutenant colonel for several years, but he provided one experience that has always stayed with me. I felt it was out of character for him—so, to me it is an aberration.

One evening in Africa, the colonel and a young Aide started drinking. I must have gone to bed fairly early, but during the night I awoke with the suddenness of an animal startled by the unusual. I lay tensely, hardly breathing, and listened to determine the nature of the confusion. I heard men breathing hard. I realized two men were struggling with each other. I listened to the grunts, the cursing, the blows and concluded the colonel and the young lieutenant had drunk too much and were fighting each other.

I found myself in a dilemma, for usually I consider myself a man of action. I am a man who recognizes the need of caution, but I have little fear of anyone. Should I go out into the darkness and try to stop the brawl?—on second thought, I decided I didn't give a damn if they killed each other.

They must have been inside the colonel's tent. I could hear the stumbling, the falling, and a thud and then—then colonel had the lieutenant down and started choking him. I could tell then the kid was struggling for life. In a gasping voice, he begged the colonel not to kill him, but the colonel continued choking him into oblivion.

Finally, I decided this was the time for action. I stepped to the door of the tent and ordered in a Texas Command voice, "Cut out this damn nonsense."

These two soldiers immediately came loose from their death grip, tried to stand, and I told them to go to sleep. The colonel started undressing and the lieutenant staggered down the street to his tent.

The next morning I went to the Mess Tent at my regular time and sat eating a leisurely breakfast. Just before the time to close the mess, the colonel walked in. He looked in excellent shape. There were a few welts on the side of his face but he had covered them pretty well.

He spoke to me in the usual manner, sat down with me at the Senior Officer table, and watched as the Aide followed him in. The Aide betrayed a sort of rough night, having some fingernail scratches on his neck. Nobody said anything but the usual. I knew that many others must have heard the hour-long battle—and I never heard another one after that.

13

I've Got Too Much Invested in That Woman

My favorite story teller had all the sharp timing, deep pathos, and fine human understanding of the best stand–up comic—except he always sat down. Armed with a beer, a light drink, or a cup of coffee, he would regale a tent full of listeners with his escapades in Brooklyn—or maybe it was in the Bronx.

He and his buddies would order cases of beer on Sunday and charge them to his mother, while she was out at mass; but he never could remember ordering them when she got the bill. His accounts of the family fights, go–rounds with the priest, and outwitting the local Irish cop on the beat were told with such horrendous imagination that when things got dull, we would get him to tell the same story again—and each time it got funnier.

The best story from my friend came when he was complaining about his wife not writing. He would tell about their courtship and everyone would be hurting from laughter—he would conclude by saying, "If I hadn't been sending all my money to that girl and didn't have so much invested in her, I would give her her walking papers." We could screech and laugh and laugh—and all during the week we'd ask him if he had received a letter. He'd answer, with his, "I've got too much invested line," and he kept it up for all the years we were in Africa and Italy.

Later one of our buddies reported—truly or falsely, I don't know, that all during the war the gal had been taking his money and spending it on some other guy. I have thought a million times about "the show must go on" for all the time our comic's heart was breaking, and he must have sensed the truth. However, he kept us in stitches and never one time let down the mask to let us know what he had surmised all along.

14

A Chaplain Takes Over

I stayed in the Army too long—or I was conditioned by my father to authority—but, at any rate, I still break into a cold sweat when I think of what happened in one of our battalions. I try to excuse the chaplain because he never had military training—and because he was a devout evangelical.

The Commanding General of the division had called a sort of debriefing session on Sunday afternoon. We had just captured Rome, crossed a high mountain, and chased the German Army across the Tiber. The Old Man wanted to point out a few bad plays and to thank the commanders for their fine work. He gave me credit for getting the Division out of Rome before our troops were captured—or completely captured—by the Italian women.

We thought we were the first U.S. Army troops into Rome. However the truth is, the American 88th (Blue Devils) Infantry Division was given a welcome by the Roman citizens that could not have been surpassed in Paris or anywhere else. They were so glad to see the Americans that they offered them every hospitality available.

I had to return to my Rear Echelon office. The next morning I drove back into Rome. Every office, every tent, the kitchen, the supply room was filled with beautiful, well–dressed and happy Italian women—and after that day, I seldom saw them again.

Our headquarters was moving at a snail's speed, and the Germans were racing to the Po River. I went into the general's office and told him we ought to move out of Rome immediately. And we, too, headed for the Po River. (This might have been funny to the general, but I got about six hundred scowls from the assembled officers—and if the exact words were repeated to the troops, I would get fifteen thousand scowls from them).

He ordered them to move out. He complained a bit about the shortage of ammunition, the condition of the vehicles—but he was proud of the fine job the men had done and he indicated his desire that this word be give to the troops at the first opportunity.

The commander of the Medical Battalion followed the general's command to a "T." He left the Division-wide formation and drove back to his Battalion area and told the adjutant to assemble the men immediately—and the men assembled. But, the colonel had overlooked or completely disregarded the fact that church was supposed to be held at this very moment.

The Battalion Commander was preparing to address the troops Sunday P.M. 6:30 and up marched the chaplain in high dudgeon. He walked up to the microphone, and without so much as a, "By your leave," the loud and authoritative voice of a modern–day Elijah with sound backing from a modern amplifier ordered, "All men who are supposed to be in church at this time fall out and assemble at the Chaplain's tent."

About one-half of the battalion fell out—and next morning the colonel was at my office, first thing. (I tried to reorient the chaplain, help the colonel, and we finally sent this aggressive man of God to an infantry battalion, where he covered himself and God with glory by his unselfishness and service.)

15

"Remember, Reuben, You've Been Thinking"

Reuben was a tall, handsome man. He had been educated in the South and had grown up in a genteel fashion. He had the Southern Gentleman's desire for a nip now and then but he never drank to excess. He had never married and I often wondered about that. He liked to come to my tent and talk, but I never found it convenient or of mutual interest to pursue his mating problems. He attended church regularly and I counted him one of my close personal friends.

He was a natural staff officer. He had the ease of conversation and the personal appearance that made him look good to generals. He talked with them in an easy manner; and he was promoted through the ranks to major, which in those days was an excellent rank.

The war finally ended in Europe, but my Southern Friend faced problems like the rest of us. We now knew how to fight a war, but few of us were prepared for the adjustments that were to take place in preparation for occupation, for fighting the war in the Pacific, and for replacing the veteran militiamen with new draftees.

I was ready to go to lunch when Reuben burst into my office, wild-eyed and almost speechless. He closed the Italian door behind me and began trying to tell me what happened. His tongue would not work. His lips were out of sync and he looked like the best candidate for a heart attack I had ever seen.

He finally calmed down enough to sit on the edge of a chair and tell me that they (the Chief of Staff and the G1) had just called him into the office and told him they were sending him down to the Leghorn to command a new battalion to take to the Pacific. "They're taking all the ack-ack boys and are going to convert them to Infantrymen—and I'm supposed to go down there and teach them how to become Fighting men. I've spent the whole war here in this headquarters. First of all, I'm not cut out to be a Battalion Commander in a Combat Regimental Team. Second, I know they just want to get me out of this headquarters and give my job to someone else."

I tried to reassure him that they thought they were doing him a favor. "I know that the Senior Staff think you are a good officer—and I know they are not trying to railroad you—and if you want to turn it down, tell them you don't want the job."

We argued about fifteen minutes—and I was getting mad because I felt he didn't think I was being honest with him. I concluded the discussion in my own typical way by saying, "Let's go down to the mess and get something to eat—and this will look different to you after lunch."

As we walked toward the mess, he told me he didn't feel like eating and would see me later. I had a good lunch and was mulling over a final cup of coffee, when one of the lieutenants ran in yelling for me, "Chaplain, come quick. Reuben has killed himself."

For a split second, I sat stunned. I had missed another boat. He wanted someone to hold onto, and in my typical Texas fashion, I had forced him to stand on his own feet—and that, at least at the moment, was the one thing he wasn't able to do. He had put his pistol to his head and pulled the trigger.

16

An Expensive Pick–Up

I grew up with the Bible in my hand. I believed every word of it even before I could read it. I believed in marriage and believed that courtship should be limited to "getting well enough acquainted to know if you wanted to marry the girl."

Acquaintance, courtship, premarital relationships had offered some real personal challenges but though with some space between beliefs and actions, I had grown into a ripe maturity with a puritanical sense of sex and sex relationships. My first military assignment was a real challenge to my philosophy of life, but I was still shocked when a British instructor, attempting to secure the somewhat irrelevant interest of a class on combat use of land mines in Africa, told a rather lurid story about an adventure with another man's wife.

At least, I wasn't ready for war, in Nazi and Fascist-Mussolini-weary Italy. I came to Italy to fight a war—and then get home as soon as possible. I soon realized that some people came to Italy for other reasons—or rather since they were there, they felt they must explore all that Italy had to offer.

One day, when an Italian girl appeared at my office door with her father, her eight–month distended pregnancy, and a load of garlic I could detect all the way across the room, I reached a new low.

She showed me the picture of the American Father (they always left an address and a picture). I never could understand it; I myself wanted to rear any kids I produced, but here the Italian father encouraged the girl to bring the *Americano* home—for he brought chocolate, American money, and some sort of prestige.

At any rate, after the couple left, I headed for the major Italian hospital. I had a wild–eyed idea. I would determine the cost of hospitalization, and the cost for rearing a child to the age of twelve—and I would force the American soldier who fathered an Italian child to pay the small amount of money needed—probably not more that $550 American dollars over a twelve-year period.

I strode into the Hospital Director's Office with my idea. The director listened patiently and then began to smile and say, "Cappelano, I suppose you have never lived in a land like this. Mussolini encouraged population growth. There is a shortage of male population around here and we have many children from our allies and our enemies. In fact, I just delivered a mother who already had six children and each of them from a different nationality of soldier. Here in this town alone we have over twelve thousand illegitimate children."

I strode out again; my Good Samaritan role had been one–upped by history.

At any rate, this aberration came from a good friend of mine. He liked women. He liked liquor. He liked me. He liked the Army and was a hard worker when he was on the job. Let's call him Jim.

Jim hit my door about bedtime. I had settled down to read the latest Religious Book of the Month—which was delivered to me regularly all during the war; but Jim broke the gap wide open between theoretical Theology and Practical Theology.

He sat down on a box beside the bed and confessed, "Chaplain, this time I'm really in trouble," and when Jim admitted he was in trouble, those who knew him, knew this was not ordinary trouble.

"You know I just got back from three days Rest and Recuperation leave in Rome. Down there I met a girl who was real friendly and she told me her folks lived in the mountains near here. She asked if she could come back with me in my jeep. She did have to lie down in the back of the jeep covered with cold weather gear when we went through two check posts. When we got up to a crossroad about a mile from here, she wanted to get out for she didn't want her folks to know she was with an American soldier.

"I was kind of glad to get rid of her. Evidently, she was an enemy agent. She tried to walk across the border and the CIC picked her up. They gave her a rough time and she confessed she came up here with me—and now, I'm going to be court–martialed for bringing an enemy agent through our lines."

At his court-martial, I testified honestly. I could say there was not malice—only sin—in his actions. We were grateful no serious security leak came from his naiveté. Jim got off with Article 15, maybe some fine—and a big black splotch on his record. I think he learned something about women from that.

17

One Part Courage

The first time I saw this character, he was a fidgety, seemingly smart-alec, rough-jawed, twenty-year-old sergeant. He literally strutted over to me. I was a visitor from "Rear" and a "Chaplain" and I felt he wanted to be sure this Greenhorn was duly impressed with his combat prowess. He had just come in from a night patrol where he had done exactly what he was supposed to have done. He and four others had gone out into the darkness into the enemy lines and quietly and efficiently picked up a German for the Intelligence Section.

I was always impressed with the plain, cold, dull courage of the infantry soldier. He went into the front line, out on the patrol, or resisted enemy attacks with a sort of resignation. (My stomach still turns a bit when I see movies where men scream and wave their arms and rush pell mell over the rampart and overwhelm the enemy.) The men I knew sat quietly, almost with foreboding, until the word came to move out. They picked up their gear, cradled their rifle in its old familiar place and moved out.

I will still give my seat or offer assistance to any Dogface who existed in Combat more than thirty days—so I didn't have to be impressed with any snow job about a patrol that goes into the mountains, sneaks through enemy mine fields and avoids enemy patrols, moves into an enemy position, isolates some enemy soldier who will know enough to make this whole deal worthwhile, capture him, get him out of enemy territory, and back into our own.

But this blond hero wanted to be sure I was fully impressed. I noted his shined combat boots as he strolled toward me. His pistol was tied down to winter woolen field pants like something from the Wild West—and this sort of made him more suspect.

"Hi, Chappie," he sang out for all to hear, almost letting his fellow soldiers know he was as brave in handling Rear Echelon Commandos as he was in dealing with the enemy. "How are things at the Rear?"

I responded in kind, informing him that, "Things are going to pieces back there. We haven't had fresh eggs for breakfast in the last two mornings," though the truth was that we hadn't had any fresh eggs for the last three hundred eighty mornings. He stopped and looked at me, and to cover any confusion, I stood and offered my hand. I introduced myself, and congratulated him on his successful patrol. I asked him to sit down.

I found that my hero was really a terrific soldier. He had been awarded every medal except the Congressional. He had been an outstanding combat soldier throughout the Italian campaign. He had led his squad well and had lost remarkably few men. He was cocky, but he was convinced there was no enemy soldier who would ever outsmart him. He read enemy defenses like a good golfer reads greens. He intuitively knew where the enemy had their machine guns hidden. He sensed enemy outposts like a foxhound trails its prey. He was a gun notcher...every time he killed a German, he put a notch on his pistol—and the handle looked like an antique.

Ray began to talk about his pistol. "When I killed my first German, I was lucky enough to get this officer. He had a P–38. I took it from him and carried it for several months during the Rome Campaign. I used my rifle most of the time. When we crossed the Tiber and headed up the Coast, we were always overrunning the enemy and they usually surrendered easily. We bypassed this farmhouse early one morning—and I decided to take a look-see. I slipped in a back door, and, sitting at a table eating his breakfast as calmly as if he were in the middle of Berlin, was a German major. My rifle was drawn and he didn't have a chance, but he jumped up and reached for his pistol. For some reason I shifted the rifle and grabbed my P–38. I shot him right in the middle and that son of a bitch kept clawing for his gun and got it halfway out of his holster. I shot him again and he still kept raising his pistol—I shot him right between the eyes—and he still fired one round when he went down. I had heard about the high velocity of the German pistol, but that thing cut through that major so fast he barely grunted. I went back and got this Army .45. Now when I hit a guy, he acts like I hit him with a baseball bat. He dies immediately and he doesn't even make an effort to pull his gun."

This man almost gleefully told me about killing six Germans in an ambush a few days before. He had set part of his squad in a prepared position on the left of a mountain trail. He and two of his men had settled inside a woodcutter's hut. The German patrol walked down the trail as if they owned it. They were chattering like kids on a picnic. At a pre-designated mark on the trail, Ray cut down the German sergeant who was bringing up the rear. The other "Tedeskis" either started running toward the other side of the valley or fell in place with their guns sputtering in some direction. The other part of Ray's squad opened up and three of the Germans fell. The two who had fallen to the ground got up and started running. Ray, claiming without any opposition from me, that he was a superb shot, calmly picked off the other two. They waited for a few minutes to see if there were any other German troops in the vicinity, then went out to be sure the enemy was dead.

One man moved and Ray fired his .45 into the groaning soldier. The .45 turned him completely over. Now they all lay still and a bit of their life blood seeped out into the white snow. By the time the echoes had stopped ricocheting around the mountains, no movement was seen.

Each man was turned over on his back. Their eyes were glassy. There was no breathing, no nervous movements to betray life. Ray concluded, "We left the poor bastards there. We saw their bodies today and they are frozen still and will stay that way till spring when we overrun their positions—and then they will be buried in American–dug graves."

I bade Ray and his cronies, "Good–night," went back into a corner of the huge building and crawled into my bedding roll. I was soon asleep, and though I am an early riser, when I awoke the next morning, Ray had already gone out with his squad to do a little scouting—and, "To pick up a few Krauts."

I left at noon to return to my headquarters, thinking I would write a book about men like Ray— but straightaway got busy and forgot both about the book and Ray.

But, Ray came back to my memory in a sudden flashing deal no more than two weeks later when I walked into a hospital ward. The Ward Sergeant called me aside as I entered the Ward. "Chaplain, drop by and see that fellow in Bed 22. He's got real troubles.

118

He has a shot through his foot—and it looks like the Powers that Be are suspicious of this sort of wound. Most guys who come in with this sort of wound shot themselves with the hope of avoiding combat. I think he deserves a little help."

I thanked the sergeant and worked my way down through the ward. Making a point to casually face the occupant of Bed 22, and lo, and behold, there before me, in GI pajamas was my Infantry Hero Ray.

I tried not to act as if I had had any advance warning and rushed over to him, shook his hand, and in a professional tone asked, "Ray, where and when did you get it?"

In real bravado, Ray commiserated, "Chaplain, I have the damnedest luck, I came in from patrol yesterday where we killed four Germans, one of them was a Captain and the other was a high ranking Sergeant. I washed up, ate a good supper and sat around cleaning up my old P–38. The damn thing accidentally went off and I blew a hole right through my foot. It messed up a few small bones, but I'll be back in Combat in a few days."

I was almost mean enough to ask Ray why he hadn't been cleaning his Army .45 rather than the German P–38, but used the Golden Rule and told him how sorry I was that this terrible thing happened.

I stopped by the Hospital Commander's tent, and told him about Ray and suggested this guy must have finally reached the point where he no longer had the guts to go out and kill Germans—but I assured him Ray had killed his share—and if it wasn't too much, ship Ray on to the Rear.

I never heard from Ray again. I don't know if they finally sent him back to the States or whether he became a Port Commando—but whatever happened, he deserved everything he got. Even a smart-alec finally gets his belly full of dead Germans—and there comes a time when the groans of dying men become indelibly impressed in the dreams of heroes—and not many sleep well with dying men—so one just can't go on and on adding groans. Sometimes he reaches his limit—and somehow, he has to get release from his terror. He keeps a brave front before others, but inside, man becomes so saturated he begins to despise his own life. A P–38 slug through the foot may be the only decent way out for a self–respecting super–hero.

18
A Christmas Tree in Combat

No one in the combat world ever saw a Christmas tree three feet tall mounted on a jeep trailer and lighted with 6–volt taillight bulbs. When I told my motor pool crew that I wanted to conduct special Christmas services in the Forward Area, this specially designed Christmas tree was operational within twenty–four hours. A special amplifier had been rebuilt to withstand the shock of combat roads. (The first time the amplifier was taken off on a trip the whole guts were shaken loose. We mounted it on springs, rubber, and finally packed the area under the resistors, condensers, and tubes with plain burlap bags and they cushioned the electrical unit so well we never had any more trouble with it.)

Eight men from Division Headquarters arranged and practiced Christmas music for a week under the direction of a graduate of the Oberlin School of Music who also served as my Section Chief, organist, typist and jeep driver.

The Adjutant General's Section printed up five thousand copies of a special program, and we headed through the mud and snow up toward the front. Wherever we found troops, we pulled up the jeep, and hoisted the lighted Christmas tree to the upright position. The folding organ was opened and a microphone placed at the sound box.

Christmas music began to fill the valleys and echo through to cold snow–covered mountains. The choir sang "Adeste Fidelis," a reader read the Christmas Story from Luke, the choir sang "Joy to the World," the Chaplain gave a brief meditation on the hope of Peace—a peace that begins in each man's heart and a peace that is possible in the midst of combat—and then a short, small soldier sang, in a beautiful tenor voice, "Away in a Manger."

Tall, gaunt, bearded, hurt men leaned on their rifles and wept unashamedly. I looked at them, standing there with eyes filled with tears—eyes that a man only sees when men have lived with death and trauma so long that the light burns out of the black orbs—and they see without seeing—they look—but with no hope.

We hauled that Christmas tree for three hundred miles and gave away all five thousand Christmas programs—and men everywhere were grateful we had come—but I doubt if those men will ever forget that little guy who sang his best tenor solo that Christmas—and I'll be one of them who remembers the Christmas tree lit up with 6–volt auto bulbs.

19

A Soldier Who Became Swiss Cheese

After church that particular Sunday night, I asked the Sergeant to get the jeep and run me by the Clearing Station for our Division Medical Battalion. I usually tried to go by once a day. These were times when the Germans had such good terrain control that only during the night was it safe to bring the wounded from the Battalion and Regimental Clearing Stations back to the rear—so I usually stopped by the hospital about two hours after sunset.

I could light a cigarette for a wounded man, give him some tea or coffee, or hot chocolate if the doctor on duty or one of the Aid Men advised it. Sometime I could carry one end of a litter and sometimes I had prayer with the dying. Though I was a Baptist, I could pray the Prayer of Absolution for a Roman Catholic, I could recite the Twenty–third Psalm for a Jew, or I could pray or read scripture to the Protestants.

Many of them who came through were not mortally wounded. They had shrapnel in a leg or arm—one man had his fanny full of mortar fragments. He happened to have his pants at half-mast at a particular slit trench when an enemy mortar round exploded nearby. I saw people with a "million dollar wound"—a good clean hole that damaged the bone and tissue enough to send a man back to the States—but not serious enough to do any long–range maiming.

But I also saw the guys who had both hands and legs blown off simultaneously by a land mine—men whose cheeks were torn off by some sort of weaponry—hand grenades, Potato Masher grenades, and the like. Some men came in with bodies as bloody as a skinned pig.

I have seen doctors working for hours removing pieces of steel from human bodies—and I've seen the same guy a few days later walking around in grand style—sort of scabby all over but in excellent spirits and grateful he was alive. I was never sure whether I should praise the skill of wonderful doctors who worked around the clock at peak combat periods to save lives—or marvel at the will of human beings to live that sometimes made bodies repair themselves when there was no hope by wonderful doctors. Or did Fate—or my God—still have things for the chopped-up body to do for the Spirit that used it for housing, for action, and for continued use?

This Sunday evening the weather wasn't too awful. I got out of the jeep in a parking area about fifty yards from the admission tent and told Van I would be ready to return to our headquarters in about an hour. That gave him time to visit some of his friends—and gave me the time I would normally spend with the wounded and with the duty personnel.

When I approached the tent, I sensed something unusual was taking place. An ambulance had just driven up and they were taking a litter into the open tent. One man rushed up to me, excitedly saying, "Chaplain, I'm glad you are here. They've just brought in a guy who is shot to pieces and he is still alive."

To say I was not too excited myself only testified to the viciousness of war, for I've seen too many men shot to pieces—but this did sound like an emergency. I pushed through the growing ring of onlookers. The doctor bent over the man recognized me and began to cut off the wounded man's uniform. He opened the sleeve and legs and gradually removed the uniform except where blood had clotted and the wool stuck to the body.

The patient whispered a few words and the doctor told me the man hadn't eaten in a few days and that I could sit by him and give him hot chocolate as often and as much as he could take. He was covered with a blanket and I held a mess kit cup of hot chocolate to his lips. At first he barely moistened his lips, but gradually he began to sip—and then his voice returned and he began to tell me the most amazing story I ever heard in combat.

Orin (the patient) had attacked the Germans four days ago. The enemy opened up with everything they had and Orin fell wounded. His buddies, those who could make it, retreated the way they had come and made it back some three hundred yards to their own dug-in positions.

Orin lay there half alive and half dead—but his half-alive portion told him he better get what life he had back to his own lines. He began to pull himself along the ground but a hail of enemy bullets kicked up all around him and pain began to eat at his whole body. He tried to move again and the hail of enemy rifle fire again engulfed him and more pains cut at him. He decided he better lie still.

The hot sun, flies and an occasional pot–shot made him wish he could run, but he lay still. He lay there that day, that night, the next day, and the next night. He had no food, no water—nothing but an occasional German bullet that cut at another part of his body.

The second night, he managed to get at his canteen for a few sips of water—but it took a medical team with a litter to get him back to our lines. He had over sixty wounds, but he also had a wonderful attitude. I guess he was moved to a major hospital and I never heard about his recovery.

20

I Hate Shadows

It was a cold November evening. The dark clouds were hanging low over the tall mountain peaks where our enemy had burrowed and settled himself in for the winter.

I walked by the chow line and a familiar but weary–acting soldier was having his mess gear filled with food. I thought he slouched over and turned toward the coffee pot when he saw me. I spoke to a few of the soldiers who were in the chow line, but kept the man at the head of the line in view. As I came closer, he pulled up his heavy trench coat till only the nose was visible and I felt he sort of ducked around the corner of the Italian school building in which we had our mess.

I went on into the officer's mess and had a nice roast beef dinner and listened to the banter and comedy that seems to go along with men as they congregate. I drank my coffee and ate my apple cobbler with a leisure that is seldom possible in most eating establishments. Mostly I listened to the conversation. There was talk of girls, wives, children, battle casualties, latest news, and prophecies about the coming winter—and a few spicy jokes that broke up the audience.

Finally I slipped out. I looked for the soldier I had seen in the chow line for there was something haunting about his appearance. But he seemed to have disappeared and I went to the office. I signed one hundred and fifty letters of condolence, trying to tell mother and fathers and wives and children something of our mutual loss in the death of their son or husband of father. I checked with the Sergeant to see if he had properly recorded the name and pertinent information of the one hundred men we had buried that day. We said an individual service for each man and tried to give them something of the dignity they deserved. I checked over the schedule for the next day and headed for my room.

My room was a private bedroom left in a nearby building that had been bombed. Parts of two walls were gone and there were no windows and the floor was leaning, but serviceable. My bed was plush: a real mattress and springs propped up on ammo boxes...I had a light bulb hanging from the ceiling that served as a reading lamp.

I sat down to pull off my boots and get set for an evening of reading. All during the war, I received a religious Book of the Month offering and all my technical magazines. Sometimes they were late in coming but I kept in touch with "the other world" and I was looking forward to a pleasant reading experience, but as soon as I sat, I heard the anti–aircraft guns open up, and I knew the Germans were pulling a sneak attack.

I snapped off the light and listened as the rumble of exploding ack-ack guns came close. New batteries took up the attack, and soon I heard the uneven chatter of the German airplane. "Washing Machine Charlie" was the name we had attached to him—though it must have been a different man each night. I think he was on an observation mission or psychologically, they wanted us to know they still had airplanes, but it was a pitiful display compared with the hundreds of bombers and fighters we sent out each day.

Charley would drop a bomb occasionally. Two nights ago he had blown up a building one hundred yards from my bedroom. Tonight he disappeared quickly and the last rumble of artillery had died out, I thought.

We were living in Monghidoro, Italy, one of these little villages that had seen only a handful of Americans till the war, but now we had taken over every extra room in the town, had pitched tents in their gardens, yards and along their roads. We had established a Troop Replacement Center at the south edge of town.

The chief attraction in the town was a church steeple that stuck up in the middle of the village like a sore thumb. The Germans could see little of the town but they could see the church tower and it became the bulls-eye for their long range guns. They had hit the top of the tower several times and the Byzantine–influenced onion on top was hanging by about 33/64 of its original wall support. All kinds of odds were laid on when it would fall, but this night after Charley made his rounds, the artillery thought they would keep us awake and they laid six heavy rounds in our vicinity. The phone did not ring so I was sure no one had been killed.

I snapped the light on and loud knocks at my precariously hanging doors brought me to the conclusion that my reading that evening would be light. I guessed it was some soldier or officer who wanted to shoot the breeze for an hour or so, but to my surprise, when I opened the door, there was the soldier that evening from the Mess Line. He still had his helmet pulled down over his eyes and his coat was pulled up high, but when he raised his head, I recognized Joe Rhoan. I had been so busy with my own visits to hospitals, cemeteries, Combat Briefings, visits to units and the conduct of three or four religious services each day that I had almost forgotten him.

Joe stood at the door, seven-eighths apologetically, and even hesitated when I asked him to come in. I asked him to pull off his coat and have a seat on the end of the bed. I lit the one–burner gasoline stove, and as I mixed up a batch of hot chocolate, I made light conversation. "Joe, it's good to see you. Where is your unit? How's your Aunt in Pittsburgh? How's the food up front? How many Purple Hearts (wounds) have you received?"

I finally poured him a cup of hot chocolate. I poured myself one, got out some stale cookies, and sat down on the bed beside him.

I watched him as he sipped the hot chocolate, and he watched me. Then, tired of the sparring, I thrust, "Joe, what are you doing back here?" Joe answered with the greatest confession a Southern Baptist Chaplain ever heard.

Joe was a beaten man. He sat huddled on the bed...his shoulders slumped. His eyes were downcast and sunken. He looked like a ten year old who had been punished and who felt the world had deserted him.

"Chaplain, I'm sorry I didn't speak to you at chow this evening, but I didn't have the guts. I thought I would bum some chow and head south. I believe I could get lost in Florence or Rome or Naples till the war is over. When I finished eating, I waited for you to come out. I saw you look around and I thought you had recognized me, so I slipped back into the darkness and prepared to catch a truck going back into the Theater Quartermaster. Those guys will give a fellow a ride for ten bucks. I was supposed to wait an hour, but the air raid hit the unloading point and destroyed several trucks and they told me nothing would be leaving until midnight. I was wandering down the street and I saw your Chaplain flag in front of your office. I went in and several of the boys were there typing and they told me where I could find you—and here I am."

I went for the jugular vein (and many people will say it was bad counseling). "Joe, what in this crazy world has happened that a guy like you would desert?"

And, like a gusher exploding from an oil well, running wild, he poured out his combat story.

Joe had been injured at the Rapido crossing. It was only a scratch, and he was proud of his Purple Heart and his combat reputation. Green soldiers envied him his experience and he gloried in the attention, but when a man has a reputation, he has to live up to it. He began to lead patrols when his outfit went into Cassino. He got promoted to staff sergeant.

He began to lead platoons in attacks. Twice he had lost every man he had, but he got the Silver Star twice and was known as the Veteran in his company, for he was one of the few Front Liners who had survived.

At Volterra, Joe won the Distinguished Service Medal. An Armored Division in front of him had been changed into Foot Sloggers by German Artillery mounted on the historic mountain. The German 88s had knocked out the majority of the American tanks and the Doughboys were called in to take the famous bastion. Joe led his company up the steep sides of the mountain so fast many of the Germans abandoned their artillery posts and were picked up by our own Reconnaissance Troops.

He was "Mister Hero" now that the Americans were fully in charge. He watched the local partisans scalp the long hair of the local Italian girls who had personally entertained the occupying German troops. He was given the key to the city and the Division Communiqués and correspondents played up his exploits. He was mentioned for the Medal of Honor, but the Division moved toward the Po so fast that the Medal of Honor turned into a DSC.

Joe slugged his way on up to the Arno and he trained his men in river assault boats for the attack across the Arno.

(I had watched the whole Division play like Marines. I saw thousands of dollars worth of assault boats being gathered for the river crossing. I never told Joe that night nor did I ever tell my Commanding General about my crossing of the Arno.

I had a Catholic priest friend, a Senior Army Chaplain with an eye for travel. One morning he came to the office and stated, "Wallace, I hear the British are moving into Florence. I want to see the city. How about going with me?"

I had never seen Florence, so I hopped into the jeep and we took off toward the Arno, traveling through the vineyards and thousand-year-old houses and castles. When we got to Florence, we found that every bridge across the Arno had been blown up by the retreating Germans, and even Father Pat Fay couldn't talk the British guards into letting us get into the line of traffic pouring over the one Bailey Bridge crossing the Allies had established.

Having grown up in a strictly disciplined home, I knew the voice of authority whenever I heard it, and I was ready to return to our own office—but Pat wasn't as easily convinced as I. We drove down the river, and three hundred yards below the Ponte Vechia were horse carts crossing the River. Pat figured the water was only two feet deep so he ordered our driver to take off his fan belt and enter the Arno.

I looked on the proceedings with deep forebodings, because this was my jeep and, if anything happened, it would be my neck—not Pat's. The Germans were still throwing in occasional rounds of ammunition to deter the pursuing British and Americans, but the shelling didn't discourage us. In five minutes, we had forded the Arno and were in the city of Florence.

Pat was wild with happiness as we paid our respects to the Cathedral with the dome that existed before Saint Peter's. We went to the Palace of the Signore and the Ponte Vecchia. We even crossed it through the rubble, and I just knew any moment a time bomb would go off. We talked with the Italians who were becoming convinced that the Germans had really gone and we were staying—but I finally persuaded Pat to get back across the Arno before we had a rain.)

Joe Rhoan remained out of combat until the 85th and 94th had knocked a hole in the mountain range between Florence and Bologna. Then his unit was thrown in—and, he commented, "It was just like fresh chuck steak tossed into an electric meat grinder. We got hell beat out of us.

"The Germans were masters of mountain warfare. Several men with one machine gun could hold off a battalion for several hours. We could take the position but would lose scores of men as we fought right up into the firing gun. When the German gunners saw they couldn't hold out any longer, they would come out with hands high over their heads with a loud surrendering 'Comarade'."

Joe went on, "We fought for every piece of high terrain. It cost us days and weeks and hundreds of men and for the first time since I hit Italy, I knew I was beginning to get Battle Rattle. Death stared at me like some buzzard waiting for a sheep to die, and sometimes without waiting, would begin to eat at the sheep's entrails before it had died. I saw so damned many guys get killed, I knew I couldn't exist much longer. At night I lay in my bedding roll and sweated, and when we got bogged down at Mount Cheri and Battaglia, I felt I couldn't take any more.

"Then word came that my regiment was setting up a special patrol unit. These guys were to make three patrols a week into German territory. They were allowed to sleep in a house, back behind a mountain that was safe from German fire. They were to have cots and their C–Rations were to be heated. I jumped at the chance and volunteered to become a Patrol Leader. I did well for a while. Maybe it was the change, but I slept better. I wasn't so afraid of being killed. But night before last it happened.

"I had orders to go out into the German area and get some prisoners for interrogation. It was pretty routine and started out well. Then I realized I was getting jumpier. I cradled my machine gun in my arms and stared into the darkness before I would proceed. I would look out there and see a form that looked exactly like a German soldier. My belly would start doing flip-flops. My heart beat about half the time and my hands were sweating like it was August—although it was really bone-chilling in the mountains. I expected any minute the Kraut would open up his 'Paper Cutter' (the name given to the German machine gun that was much like our Thompson but it clattered when fired). I would ease up to the figure with my machine gun ready to fire and I would finally get close enough to kick it—and I found it was a bush. Well, that night I had already kicked ten bushes and was at the point of emotional exhaustion.

"I will hate shadows all my life; I even dodged them tonight as I came down here. Then one of my men stepped on a land mine. The explosion tore him to pieces and killed two fellows who were too close to him, but the Germans heard and saw the flash—and in ten seconds, we were penned inside the worst mortar box I have ever seen. Once they found a target, they laid their explosives down so they surrounded us with walls of exploding mortar rounds. Then they began to methodically chunk artillery shells into the center of their square. Men were screaming, running, praying, and out of twelve men, only three of us finally broke out and got back to our own lines.

"Chaplain, I admit I was terrified. I tried to look calm, but I couldn't eat, couldn't sleep, and for the first time in my life I didn't know what to do. Death perched over me like an old buzzard—and I could see Death all night and all day.

"This morning they told me I was to lead a patrol tonight. I prayed. I walked out by myself and cried. This afternoon I told the lieutenant I was going down to draw ammunition for tonight's patrol—and instead of drawing ammo, I just kept going.

"I came by your headquarters and knew I could bum a meal and you know the rest."

Tears poured down my face as I looked at this kid. I thought about Oklahoma, the boat trip over, Casablanca and now, I thought about his aunt and about the fifteen thousand other guys just like him in my own division. I thought of divisions flung across the boot of Italy, about Stalingrad, Guadalcanal. I'm not a very sentimental man, but what religion I have is real. I took hold of Joe's hand and I asked him about his religious faith. I prayed that God would help him and us meet this problem; and I honestly felt that if I ever needed Divine help I had to have it now.

In the quietness of the night the big guns began booming again, and Joe acted like he was under attack. He began by saying, "I know my patrol is out there. I know they are being mauled to pieces and I have failed them. I've ruined my life and I'll never be able to right this thing I've done."

I settled down and turned to him, "Joe, you can keep running if you want. I guess there are many American soldiers who are sacked in with some Italian family. I presume they can stay there the rest of their life if they want to—but I don't believe any man can run away from life. No matter where you go, your past will be looking over your shoulder. I think you ought to go back to your unit. I'll give you a note to give your commander."

Joe seemed relieved and I typed out a note.

"Commander, Ranger Patrol
Dear Sir;
I have spent the evening talking with Joe Rhoan. I have known him since Camp Gruber days and I am convinced he has become saturated with combat. He has almost lost his nerve and came down to see me with the full intention to keep going. I suggest he be given a change and moved to a less stringent combat situation. I will be in to see you in the morning.

Sincerely,
Chaplain Hale
Division Chaplain, Hq.88th Infantry Division"

I signed the note and sealed it, without telling Joe what I had written. I dressed, went to the Motor Pool and got my jeep and took Joe back to within one half mile of his patrol base. I drove back to Monghidoro, checked in my jeep, and crawled into bed.

The next morning I got up early, read a bit, grabbed a good breakfast, and headed to the office. I got the work going and called my driver to get the jeep ready to go up the front. The words had not been uttered one minute and my office door burst open and there stood Joe Rhoan.

His eyes were bright and he stood tall, and he looked like the old Joe Rhoan. He was a miracle. He looked like a guy who had been born again, and he was bubbling. He didn't mind that the office was filled with men and he just blurted out, "Chaplain, when I got back last night and told Lieutenant Waverly I had almost gone over the hill and I showed him your letter—I expected him to put me under arrest—but he was really kind. He told me I should have confided in him. I should have told him I couldn't take any more combat—he understood what it means when you have a bellyful of this sort of stuff. He told me he would have moved me back to a less exposed situation. But, now, I don't want to move. I want to be with my men and use my experience and my knowledge to get this thing over."

I told Joe how happy I was and wished him well. He left and when he closed the door, I called his outfit and talked with the lieutenant. I thanked God he was the sort of man who understood men's hearts and knew what it meant to forgive and walk the second mile with his troops.

One month later I buried the same lieutenant, and for weeks I woke up crying in my sleep. "Why do good men like this die so soon? Why do the bums and the cowards and the emotionally immature escape responsibility; and are allowed to spend their lives decrying the efforts of those who protect their rights to be bums and cowards and emotionally immature?"

Lieutenant James Waverly was typically Joe College in the best sense of the term. He had played football at Centenary in the days when oil millionaires loved the little Shreveport school. He had spent his summers working on oil rigs and he had muscles to prove it. He was a smart Joe College, but he had the Southerner's charm and patience with his fellow human beings.

Jim had been handpicked for the Ranger Patrol unit but his value to the Regiment had been so great that the Regimental Commander finally decided he was needed in one of the companies looking right into Bologna.

Jim landed in his company one morning about nine o'clock and by noon every man in the company had been recognized as a person by him, and he had been promoted to Captain. He moved quietly but effectively from one squad to another, from one section to another and within three days the Company was his; and in one week he was ordered to move out on the mountain promontory that punched out like an arrowhead into the German army's side.

The newly placed Infantry Company took stock of its position and realized they were as vulnerable as a triple—stacked ice cream cone in a Texas noonday sun. They reinforced their position as quickly as they could–and none too soon.

Snow was beginning to fall at the edges of the Apennines and the Krauts were fearful that some eager commander might punch a hole through their defense positions and decide to winter in the Po Valley, and since Italy was so much better than the Stalingrad front, they were willing to pay quite a price to keep the line intact. So, to keep the American front from becoming too confident, and having a good eye for dangerous terrain, they decided to shake up our boys on the threatening arrowhead; to do this they launched an attack in force.

Captain Jim's troops had thrown up sand bags in strategic locations, oiled their weapons, and they watched the combined snow and fog drift toward their position. The Krauts were watching, too, and, about the time the fog arrived, they launched a full-scale attack on every company position on the mountain.

Jim was not caught by surprise.

He heard the first shot come out of the fog and he moved from position to position encouraging his men; and his men performed gallantly. Their machine guns and rifles spewed death at anything that moved in the fog and snow flurries to their front. They made the Germans pay for their aggressiveness—but they had not counted on Kraut stubbornness. They fired all day and into the night—and the enemy still kept coming. Occasionally there was a hand-to-hand encounter as some German soldier slipped into a defense position. By morning, the ammunition was dwindling to a serious level, and it was hard in those days to get door-to-door delivery.

At daybreak, the Germans launched a suicidal attack. Captain Jim saw and felt the main force of the assault. He grabbed a machine gun off a tripod and took it into the midst of the fight. The gun got so hot he couldn't hold it and sat down on the frozen ground and held the gun between his legs and fired down the mountain.

The firing finally ceased, and the mountains became quiet. The few Germans who were alive dragged themselves back to their holes somewhere below. Americans began to look at the havoc around them. Then someone noticed that the new company commander was not around—and they found him twenty feet out in front of the first position. He lay on his back in the light snow, his body riddled with enemy machine gun fire. His own dead machine gun still lay between his legs—and he only had ten rounds left in his belt.

The company was stunned, but in four hours they had a new company commander—but no matter how good he was, he would lack some of the good things I saw in Jim Waverly.

I buried him in a cemetery that now filled a whole valley. His cross looked like all the rest, but he will always represent the finest company leadership and he was one of the four bravest men I ever knew—and I think he was the most human.

21

The End's in Sight

Margaret Burke White came to Italy that last winter to take pictures of our combat soldiers for a national magazine. She lived with our troops at the front, struggled through the snow and became acquainted first-hand with the feeling of being wet and cold for three months at a time. She eventually returned to Naples, got out of her jeep, went in to touch base with her news staff, came back out and some petty thief had stolen every combat negative she had left in a box in her jeep.

She immediately returned to the combat area to the same outfit, but by then, the snow was beginning to melt and we were getting ready to launch an attack toward Bologna.

We sat in front of Mount Rumici, and when they rang the bell, our troops swept across the plains, along the river banks, up the valleys and by daylight we had won our objectives. To the right and left, our allied divisions had also won their objectives. We hit the second objective and were on our way to the Po Valley.

The Germans were routed and the poor devils tried to make it across the Po River. Their convoys were strung out for miles and their foot soldiers either walked along roads or boarded trucks, but they, by the thousands, flowed toward the main bridge across the Po.

But, for the first and only time, I saw our Air Force do what they claim to do in the movies. They ranged along the roads strafing and bombing, and this time they were good shots. They destroyed vehicles by the thousands, and the dead Germans were stacked like cordwood in the ditches along the miles of road.

I tried to imagine the weary German infantrymen slogging along the roads, long single lines on either side of the road. Someone yelled air attack and they fell into the ditches along the road—and our planes strafed them as they lay in the ditches.

I have seen them three deep dead in the ditches.

I never looked at a dead man's front and back that I did not put myself in his place. He wanted to go home. I thought about his unborn children, his unrealized hopes, and his earthly unfulfillment. I believe in life hereafter, but I know this earth is the testing ground for eternity. I never minded the battle, and earthly failure hurts only a little while—but when you are dead this chapter is closed—and I've never been intent in doing the next chapter until I finish what God wanted me to do in this one.

A few Germans got across the Po and others were stationed north of the river. Our troops were relentless. One of our outfits marched over fifty miles in a little more than twenty–four hours, and they began to sweep northern Italy like a housewife with a broom. Our troops met spasmodic resistance and our casualties were heavy at times.

I caught up with Joe Rhoan at Vicenza, and to my amazement he was now a lieutenant. He was commanding an infantry company and was waiting for transportation that would take him up the other side of the mountain and cut off German troops who were trying to make it over the Brenner Pass. They had been spotted by our aircraft and Joe had been hand–picked for the job.

He assured me he was doing fine. His new lieutenant from the Ranger Patrol had been selected to take a company into the spring offensive and he had recommended Joe to become the Ranger Patrol commander. He was commissioned a second lieutenant before the Spring Drive and a week later had inherited the company after a captain and a lieutenant had been killed and there were no trained replacements to take over.

Joe, in good command fashion, had a vat of hot coffee and huge bologna sandwiches available for his men. He and I sat down on a nearby park bench in the center of the old city and talked for an hour.

His unit had not run into any heavy increments of Krauts since they let the Mountains south of the Po, but, as he described his march northward, I thought of Sherman's march to the sea. They had killed everything in a German uniform that moved. He talked about the effectiveness of his troops much as I would have talked about killing flies in the Company mess hall. He claimed that since they left the mountains, his one hundred fighting men alone had killed a thousand of the enemy.

Joe began with their wild race to the Po. They stole, borrowed and utilized every sort of transportation they could get, and within a mile of the bridge, they caught up with the tail of the German column. The Germans weren't putting up much of a fight; they were trying to get across the bridge.

As Joe's men closed in, some German gave the command to blow the bridge and it went sky high. "German troops were blown sky high," Joe exhilarated, "by their own troops. The rest of the enemy troops on the south side tried to swim across, tried to surrender, but few tried to fight. We set up our machine guns and we killed everything that moved. Then we took pot shots in the water and those who weren't drowned by the swift waters, we killed. I finally stopped the men for I was scared. I saw my own men killing those who were on their knees begging for their lives. One German had jumped into the water with a full field pack and when he started sinking, he crawled back to shore. He didn't have a gun that we could see and as he walked toward the bank with his arms high over his head, one of my men emptied a clip right into his gut. I'll never forget the look on his face. He acted as if he had been sure no American would do such a thing.

"I thought of all the damnable things Germans had done to the Poles and Czechs, and my first reaction was to kill every bastard in a German uniform, but I had noticed the Germans were getting older and older and younger and younger. I knew Hitler was scraping the bottom of his manpower barrel—and I told my men to lay off those poor son-of-a-bitches. But by that time there weren't many left."

Joe recounted how the engineers had taken his main combat strength across the river in combat boats. Their jeeps and trucks and artillery were to follow as soon as the long pontoon bridge was in operation, for before we left, the engineers were already there with equipment and supplies to build a pontoon bridge and to try to bridge the remains of the old structure.

Joe got over a hundred men across the river and they were soon being joined by other troops and they began the fifty-mile race to Trento. They barely slept or ate and they hit the city just after daybreak.

"Sitting around a truck column, were several companies of Jerriers," Joe Rhoan reported. "Those sons-of-bitches were sitting there eating their breakfast like there wasn't an American in one hundred miles. They were shouting, pushing each other, and having a helluva time. They didn't have an idea they were surrounded. When we opened up on them with rifles and submachine guns, the damn' fools didn't even know where their weapons were and most of them died with their face in their morning cereal.

"We took their trucks and headed toward Vicenza, and, by this time, the scared bastards were caught between us and the British and we were chewing them up by the droves."

Joe's ragtail bunch had gotten in that night and got their first real sleep in seventy–two hours. Their own trucks came in for breakfast and they were ready to move north as quickly as the convoy came to transport the Doughboys for no infantry company in those days was self-supporting.

I settled down and listened to Joe.

"When we hit Rome, I was close enough to the first combat troops that when my driver and I rode through the streets, it was like a carnival. People lined the streets at least ten deep. Pretty girls threw kisses, older women were more obvious and the men shouted 'Viva America'.

"I drove down to our Forward Echelon in the Northern part of the city and saw a commotion on the Tiber River. I could see a man trying to crawl out of the river, but people lined up on the banks would kick him back in. He would struggle down stream another ten feet and someone else would kick him in. I watched this gruesome thing for ten minutes and finally the man drifted away from the bank, struggled a few times and sank.

"I couldn't believe what I had seen for it was impossible for more than a dozen men of all those hundreds lining the bank to know this man. I turned to some Italians, and in my First Grade Italian, I inquired what was going on and they told me this was a German sympathizer."

I had run into a similar situation a few days later. I had an office in a lovely building and had the nicest window in town. It overlooked the village piazza and I spent much time watching the people, listening to their conversation and still marveling at their spirit.

One afternoon I heard a ruckus outside my window and I saw a hay cart being drawn by men and accompanied by at least five hundred of the local gentry. It reminded me of something out of a French Revolution as they spat upon a man and a woman in the hay cart. They had their hands tied behind them. There was a sort of resignation in their eyes. Both were bloody and had been smeared with horse dung. Little children and old women and old men and adolescents screeched at them. People threw all sorts of objects at them and several times they were shaken by stones that struck them and brought more blood.

Whether or not this mob saw an American colonel standing in a window—or whether by chance, or whether they knew the local jail was just behind my building, they did stop the cart in front of my window and began to tell me this pair had betrayed their country and ought to be killed. A fellow in a uniform took down one of the stakes on the hay cart and pulled the man off. He fell on the ground and I saw that his arm had been broken at the elbow and the bone was sticking through the skin, but before he had hardly hit the ground, people began to kick him and stomp him—and I did the most ridiculous thing I ever did in my life.

Without thinking, I stood to my six-foot height, combat boots and all, and I jumped eight feet down to the ground in the midst of all this frenzy. I took hold of the prisoner and held him against the wall. I told the mob that they were the ones who were cowards. They should put this man in jail and try him when their minds were clear. If he deserved death, kill him, but do it legally.

I stormed at them to go home and take care of their own families and I called a local *carbineri* who had been standing on the sidelines and told him to take these two people to jail.

Surprisingly, the mob broke up and in ten minutes the piazza returned to normalcy.

The next day a soldier from our Recon Crew told me about some partisans who wanted our boys to fire on a house about a hundred yards from the road. The Partigani said there were some criminals in there. My Recon man said he wouldn't shoot until he knew who was in the house.

He drove his armored car up to the house and shouted for the occupants to surrender. An old man and woman in their eighties came out with their hands up. Our troops entered the house and found no one else, and concluded that the Partigani really wanted to take what the old couple had saved and probably stored in some part of the house.

Joe sat and listened and he got the message. Our troops were beginning to think and act like the people we fought. He must have chewed on his sandwich for five minutes, then he said, "Chaplain, I tried to show you about how mean we were. We did all the things I said we did, but we aren't proud of them. I have seen men enter a house and walk across a beautiful sofa with their muddy boots.

"The other day one of my men had a long lever and was tearing down a chimney. I asked him what the Hell he was doing, and he admitted he didn't know...he just wanted to tear the damn thing down.

"When I was a little kid, I used to knock the window panes out of abandoned houses and used to shoot insulators off telephone poles. I justified the latter because I wanted to be a good shot and the insulators made good targets, but I think I broke the windows because I wanted to hear the clash of breaking glass.

"Chaplain, I hate what I have become. There are times I like to kill. It gives me a sense of superiority; but there are times I know I have lived longer than my time. I was so sure when I came by to see you in Monghidoro that I would have been killed if I had gone out on that patrol that night; I don't get much sleep because I have horrible dreams.

"When I was on R&R in Rome and should have been resting, every time I went to sleep I had nightmares. In my dreams, all the men I had killed came marching by and I could look beyond their line of march and see weeping women and old men and occasionally they would scream out when their son or husband marched by—and kept on marching out of sight. I drank heavily for the first time in my life. I took on women till I was exhausted—and finally came back to my outfit a day early, because I couldn't take any more Rest and Recuperation.

"I have been driving my men ever since. They don't sleep any more than I do and we will be glad when this thing is over; but all of us wonder how we are going to make it if they tell us that now we are finished here, we have to go over and fight the Japs. I think—"

And I never knew what he thought, for the convoy of trucks hove into sight. Joe shook hands, saluted and got his men aboard. He went by every truck yelling, "This is our chance to finish every damn German in Italy. This is the last time around."

Joe crawled into his jeep at the head of the column, pulled his arm up to its full height and gave a forward motion. The convoy rolled forward and disappeared on the mountain road climbing toward the summit. I didn't know I had heard Joe talk for the last time—and less did I know that the next time I would talk to Joe he wouldn't hear.

The beefed-up Infantry Company moved toward Brenner Pass and their strategy was perfect. The German column was under observation by our aircraft and Joe set up his ambush at the best location possible. He placed a road mine, which blew up the lead vehicle in the German convoy; Joe yelled for the Krauts to surrender—but there was one thing an aircraft observer could not tell Joe.

This convoy carried an elite S.S. Regiment. These were Hitler's choice fanatics, and because of their sense of honor to each other, they began to fight. Stupid S.S. men tried to play Superman and strode toward the Americans with machine guns blazing like something out of a war movie. The Americans mowed them down like clover. They mortared them, fragged them, got them with potshots and machine-gunned them into oblivion.

When the shooting stopped, not one S.S. Trooper was alive and there was one dead American. Joe Rhoan had caught a bullet right in the middle of his forehead.

Joe's first sergeant called me and told me he was bringing Joe's body back to the cemetery. One of our hot-shot Piper Cub pilots flew down and landed me in an alfalfa field—and we almost lost our lives on the take–off as the plane wheeled into an irrigation ditch that had been hidden by the green hay.

I walked about a half mile to the cemetery and there sat the sergeant and one of the Graves Registration personnel. Some Italian workmen had just finished the grave.

I walked over to the mattress cover, untied the top and there was Joe. He was as peaceful as a child asleep, and except for the round red–rimmed hole in his forehead, he looked every inch the man he had become; except now he was dead and the war in Italy was finished.

He no longer had "Battle Rattle."

I tied up the mattress cover, motioned for the Italian workers to follow me and the first sergeant to the grave, where they took a couple of woven lines and let his body down into the depths. He lay there as I read the burial service.

I tested my own faith with every sentence and I tested my world. "I am the resurrection and the life, he that believeth in me, though he were dead, yet shall he live: and whosoever liveth and believeth in me shall never die. Our help———"

I committed his body to the ground and—as best a Protestant can, I commended his soul to Eternity and to God. I threw in a handful of dirt and then took a shovel. The first sergeant and I covered him up while the Italians stood there, wondering about those crazy Americans doing the menial job that they had been paid to do.

POSTLUDE

Men fight because, at that moment, they see no other chance for survival or because they are the sort of people who want to take what they want from weaker people.

I have never fought a war of aggression where our country wanted to take land or possessions or freedom from anyone else. Most of the fighting I have known came about because some big bully was trying to dominate one of the smaller people who were our friends.

In a real sense, war only gives those who survive another chance to solve their problems in a better way than they were solved when the war started.

In years of consideration, I have concluded that some men would rather get theirs by force. Other men would rather get theirs by work. As long as there are men who abuse force, this world will need policemen, Texas Rangers, and international policemen or soldiers. I long for One World and a real United Nations—but until that time we will be sending our Joe Rhoans to war. I fought wars against Hitler and his henchmen; I fought against Tojo and Japan and their militaristic thugs. I fought against North Korean dictatorships and against North Vietnamese aggression. We must continue to protect our families from anyone who would enslave us.

Rev. Wallace M. Hale

I have met a few men who express a deep patriotic philosophy, but I have met thousands who willingly give their lives to assure a good life for their families and their homes for future generations. Our Fallen Comrades did give their lives for America and we must continue their war against oppression and slavery. We are grateful for their sacrifice. We are proud to have served with them, and to their Loved Ones, we continue to offer ourselves in support of our Nation.

THE DEAD STILL SPEAK
Chaplain (Col) Wallace M. Hale
(originally published in Blue Devil,
our division newspaper
on May 30, 1946)

Dead men are hard to carry but I was impatient as I waited for the soldiers to bring another body. I looked into the mud that oozed and sloshed around my boot tops and could think only of the hurt and refuse and nastiness of real war. I was plain sick and tired of the whole business—no, not sick of burying those dead—just sick in heart and soul and gradually growing numbed to everything that did not help me and my boys keep living.

I meditatively scanned the cold, cruel hunk of rock that raised its boasting bold head over the U.S. Military Cemetery and I felt the driving wind pulling at my parka and peeking into my good old 'long handles'. "Oh, God—it's cold in Italy." I began to feel warmer as I moved my thoughts from the Apennines to warm, nice days in Texas when my brothers and I were too young to know or care about this country—when we laid in the green grass and soaked up the wonderful rays of a friendly sun. How different today with those boys up there in the mountains, transported to a foreign country by the inroads of a tyrant fighting an enemy that is tough, good, and stubborn. Yesterday they were mere kids, farmers, salesmen, husbands, sons—but today...

Here they came with a body. Four Italian soldiers, one on each corner of a litter, staggering through the mud and mire, trying to walk reverently, but almost deterred from their purpose by the slippery, heavy mud and dead weight of their precious cargo. "Oh God, how precious." "An American soldier, saying good-bye to the world, dressed in a shroud" (as the Army called it). Everyone was dressed that way—Generals, Colonels, Lieutenants, Sergeants, and Privates. That was the way a "combat soldier" went through. I have heard of a few high rankers who got a box but I wouldn't want one—I'd hate to try to explain to the dead all around me why I was different.

The quartet moved into the row and staggered into the narrow opening between the graves. They set the litter down, and with an efficiency, betraying long and much practice, they placed the two ropes—one under the armpits and one under the bend of the knees. Someone bailed water from the grave. The soldiers tugged at the ropes, lifted the body clear and let it swing dizzily, but easily, into the tomb—a grave dug out of rock. There was no easy digging in these mountains—even foxholes were hard to dig.

I stepped up to the grave with my New Testament, opened it at the proper place as the soldiers on my left withdrew and folded their muddy, sticky ropes. All activity became subdued and onlookers removed their hats—in spite of the rain that had begun to blow through the passes—in spite of the fact that the temperature was almost freezing. Suddenly, I could hear the muffled, mountain-stifled booming of our Artillery, as I glanced toward the familiar rows of new graves to the knolls that hemmed us in. A few days ago we were fighting on this very hill. The hell of crashing mortars, the disciplined condensed rat-tat-tat of the machine guns, the booming, ground-shaking heavy stuff, the spat of the rifle, and the groans and agony of wounded and dying. With their spilled blood, they had made this valley as sacred and hallowed as the ground on which Moses met God.

My stomach seemed empty and glued to my backbone. My intestines groaned as my emotions demanded the extra juices for my stomach. My heart hurt and my lips were so dry I had to moisten them. I was the one who was to say the last good-bye to this man who had died so far from where he had intended to die. I forgot the people as I looked into the grave at the shrouded form. How strong he must have been. There was scarcely room for his broad shoulders. He was tall, too, a 6-foot regulation grave was almost too short. Only a few days ago, he was alive like I am now. He feared, he sang, he prayed, he dreamed. He wanted to go home and he loved his wife like I love mine. He loved and was loved, he had hopes for tomorrow and yearned for the days he would be out of Khaki and ODs. He didn't like war. He was a civilian at heart though he and the millions like him made the best soldiers the world had ever seen. But all that is finished now. He won't go back. He's dead. His lips are mute, his body is cold, he's finished, or is he?

Then came the revelation that I had not dreamed possible, the three thousand men

I thought dead actually became active in humanity's climb upward. Heretofore, I had pronounced them dead but they became alive as I prayed the last prayer—"Our Gracious Heavenly Father who made the World and all of us thy children, Thou who understandeth our frailties, our mistakes, our problems. Wilt Thou deal mercifully with this thy son who has so abruptly come to Thee? Give him the best that Thy justice and mercy can offer and be with us who remain behind (There I heard the Voices) and, wilt Thou especially bless his loved ones who will be so saddened when they hear of his passing. Give them strength and courage to carry on. Give them wisdom and faith to live purposefully and sacrificially. They have given enough. In the name of our Savior who taught us to pray, we ask these things—Amen."

When I finished the prayer, I slowly opened my eyes. There was the mud, and the cold and the war,—but there was the chorus of the men I had thought dead. "Chaplain, we have carried the torch this far. None of us were ready to cash in our chips but here we are. Few of us were gallantly patriotic, but we did love America.

"We loved our home and our way of life; and, deep down, we would rather have this than the slavery the enemy would have imposed upon us and our loved ones. We have done all we can, except as we live through you and others like you. Here's the torch; we give to all who can bear it. May you never forget our beckoning and may you and America succeed where we and tens-of-thousands have failed.

That happened a long time ago—but the dead still speak to me. I can still see the rows and lines of graves. I see the strained but jovial faces of these men as they lived and I see their shrouded forms as they lay dead—but I hold on to my torch and try to lift it high enough that it might challenge someone who hadn't seen it before.

END